What People Have Said about the PDC Transformation

A Board member and shareholder of PDC

"From the Board's point of view, the PDC transformation was a vital gamble at a time of very high uncertainty. We worried that the organization was close to the brink, and wondered whether it would survive the requisite changes. Sergio believed that investing in organizational structure would provide the foundation for rebuilding a stronger and more resilient organization. The transformation gamble has generated remarkable shareholder value, and has positioned our company for continued growth."

- Salvador Paiz, Chairman of the Board, PDC

A customer: consumer products company that buys PDC's sales and distribution services

"The inspiring transformation of Grupo PDC resonates with everyone who feels part of this wonderful project.

"For LA SIRENA, Guatemala represents an example of working with a committed distributor. In the past 10 years, we have doubled sales, strengthened our leadership in the Sardines category, and achieved leadership in the Tuna category.

"We hope to continue replicating this same success story, from Guatemala to El Salvador, and soon in Peru. We remain committed to growing with Grupo PDC. I can only thank you for all the dedication in becoming the best distributor in Latin America!"

- Lorena Ruiz, Sales and Marketing Director LATAM,
Otis McAllister

A customer: retail chain that buys PDC's consumer goods

"From my side, there is nothing left but to congratulate you for modernizing, formalizing, and professionalizing the entire PDC team. Thanks to this and a clear strategic vision, you have achieved an extremely solid CAGR [compound annual growth rate], consolidating yourselves as a strategic business partner for Unisuper.

"I have no doubt that the future will continue to show the fruits of this great work."

- Francisco Mugica, CEO, Unisuper

One of PDC's bankers

"Bam Guatemala, an affiliate of Bancolombia, partnered with PDC as a lead structuring agent of a unique acquisition funding facility to fuel its growth, largely because of PDC's commitment to integrity and an unparalleled reputation for operational excellence."

- Federico Bolaños, General Manager, Bam Guatemala

Another executive: a CEO who was inspired and guided by PDC's story

"Meeting Sergio Paiz at a Great Game of Business conference was an important step in 1st Pet Veterinary Center's growth. Sergio shared the story of the success that he had with Dean Meyer's principles of organizational structure. He has built an impressive people-first business.

"We had been an ESOP for just over a year, and had successfully played the Great Game for two years before that. His example opened my eyes to what more is possible, and what more we needed to do.

"We followed the same path. Like Sergio, we threw our old organization chart out the window and created a brand-new organization based on Meyer's principles.

"This journey has provided us with clarity, and it has given true ownership of their internal lines of business to our leaders. Through this process, we are driving the entrepreneurial spirit down to each of our team members who care directly for our pet patients and our clients. This has taken pressure off of me, as our leaders are now empowered and aligned with their accountabilities. It has been an exciting process that gives me much hope for our future.

"I love Sergio's book because it shows how great things can happen when correct principles are followed. I recommend it to any CEO who is interested in developing an organization that just works."

– Dr. Randy Spencer, CEO, 1st Pet Veterinary Center
(a multi-hospital pet health care system)

Another executive: a shared-services leader who is applying these concepts in local government

"This book brought to life the concept of a business-within-a-business organization. Seeing how it played out across teams, regions, product lines, support functions, and acquisitions gave me a clear sense of how it drives accountability and scale, especially in more complex organizations.

"One thing that really struck me was how internal customer-supplier relationships can shift the way teams see themselves – not just as departments fulfilling tasks, but as service providers with clear deliverables and ownership. That felt especially relevant to our own organization, even in a public-sector context.

"I'd add that i t was an enjoyable read. Sergio's openness about the chaos he stepped into, and the toll it took on him personally, made the transformation feel real and grounded – not just another polished success story. It's a great case study. It definitely sparked many insights and opportunities for me."

– Berke Attila, Director,
Baltimore City Department of General Services
(Energy, Facilities, Fleet, Finance, HR, and
Performance Management)

Another executive: a CIO of a small IT department, who found this example equally relevant

"I just finished my second reading of this book. What a story of transformation! Really inspiring!

"Some of the feelings Sergio talked about when becoming CEO were the feelings I had when first taking on my job. Although PDC is a company and we are an IT department, and we're tiny compared to them, many of the problems he discussed were similar to those I inherited. And the same organizational principles apply.

"We are following a similar path, applying Meyer's business-within-a-business approach. And we, too, are seeing remarkable results. I will probably read this book a few more times, picking up additional nuances each time I do. Great work, Sergio!"

– Lee Gerney, CIO, Yolo County, California

Employees' perspective: a top executive at PDC

"Throughout my career, I experienced several massive restructuring processes where the fundamental principles of organizational design were ignored. The consequences were devastating, both for the company and its employees. They resulted in talent desertion, and destroyed the culture.

"Being part of this transformational process from the beginning has been one of the best experiences in my career. This framework has given us a scientific way to build a world-class organization of empowered and committed entrepreneurs."

– Carlos Alberto Penagos Serovic, Brand Management Lead, PDC

Employees' perspective: a senior manager at PDC

"Before joining PDC, I worked in a matrix structure with two or more bosses, each of whom defined their priorities and focuses (normally not aligned with each other). It was hard on me, and ultimately it didn't work.

"At PDC, we are empowered; and priorities are clear (generally set by our internal customers). It's a high-performing organization, and a really great place to work!"

– Pedro Luis Marroquin, Engineering Lead

Employees' perspective: a (former) employee at PDC

"My 5 years working at PDC made a real difference in my professional and personal career. Having worked in two companies since then, I can tell you that PDC is light-years ahead. I'm succeeding in these other companies using what I learned at PDC.

"I can also tell you that PDC is special in its human quality – a focus on the well-being of people. That generates real commitment.

"PDC is a benchmark in the industry, and is making a difference to so many people. A lot of companies can learn from you. I'm proud to have been a part of PDC, and hope someday (if the opportunity arises) to be able to contribute what I've learned outside back to my PDC family."

- Luisa García Urzúa

An internationally respected organizational design consultant

"If you are interested in organizational design, I recommend this book. It chronicles an amazing story of the rebirth of a family business on the verge of collapse through organizational transformation.

"I loved the first-person story that CEO Sergio Paiz tells. The narrative is captivating and inspiring, taking you through the journey from the mess he inherited, to what he did (in detail), why he did it, and the outcomes and benefits; and the benefits (and business results) are impressive.

"This is a great case study with lots of lessons and provocative thinking."

- Dr. Paul D. Tolchinsky, founder and former chair,
European Organisational Design Forum

Every Manager an Entrepreneur

How PDC implemented the business-within-a-business organization, and the remarkable results

Sergio Paiz

EVERY MANAGER AN ENTREPRENEUR

How PDC implemented the business-within-a-business organization, and the remarkable results

Paiz del Carmen, Sergio

Key words: leadership, organization, structure, transformation, scalability, agility, empowerment, entrepreneurship, intrapreneurship, acquisitions integration, teamwork, employee engagement.

NDMA Publishing, N. Dean Meyer and Associates Inc. Ridgefield, CT, 06877 USA.
www.ndma.com
ndma@ndma.com

ISBN:

English, hard-cover book: 978-1-892606-36-5
English, paperback book: 978-1-892606-40-2
English, Kindle: 978-1-892606-37-2
Spanish, hard-cover book: 978-1-892606-38-9
Spanish, paperback book: 978-1-892606-41-9
Spanish, Kindle: 978-1-892606-39-6

Dedication

To my wife Paulina and children, Alexandra, Sergio, Stephanie, and Mati.

Your patience, love, and unwavering support carried me through the many years of late nights, long trips, and difficult decisions.

I could not have led this transformation without you.

Thank you for standing by me, even during the moments when I wasn't fully present.

Contents

Preface 1

Foreword (by N. Dean Meyer) 3

Introduction 5

1. A Bit of Personal History First 9

2. What I Inherited 15

3. What I Did: The Triage Phase 23

4. Transformation To What? 29

5. The Challenge of Multi-business, Multi-country 41

6. Our Design: A Fully Integrated Company 51

7. Transformation Strategy 63

8. Principle-based Approach to Structure 71

9. Our Restructuring Process 77

10. Cross-boundary Teamwork 87

11. Business Results So Far 93

12. Example of Benefits: Talent 97

13. Example of Benefits: Customers 109

14. Example of Benefits: Innovation 115

15. Example of Benefits: Acquisitions 117

16. Example of Benefits: External Sale of Support Services 129

17. Example of Benefits: Reputation 133

18. Where We Are Now 137

19. Words to the Wise 143

Endnotes 151

Biography: Sergio Paiz 156

Figures

Figure 1: What Entrepreneurs Do 30

Figure 2: The Impacts of Employee Engagement 36

Figure 3: Fully Integrated Organizational Design 55

Figure 4: Dimensions of the Cube 59

Figure 5: Five Organizational Systems 65

Figure 6: Entrepreneurial Metrics 70

Figure 7: Seven Principles of Structure 75

Figure 8: Types of Internal Businesses:
The Building Blocks of Structure 79

Figure 9: Our Rainbow Organization Chart 80

Figure 10: Definition of High-performance Teamwork 88

Figure 11: Steps in a Walk-through 90

Figure 12: Our Sales Growth 94

Figure 13: Our Employee Mobile App 103

Figure 14: Employee Engagement Results 106

Figure 15: Brand Positions by Country 113

Figure 16: Most Acquisitions Fail to Deliver Expected Value 118

Figure 17: Growth in the Australian Dairy Business 124

Figure 18: The Difficulty of Starting New Businesses 131

Every Manager an Entrepreneur

How PDC implemented the business-within-a-business organization, and the remarkable results

Preface

This book tells the real story of how Grupo PDC implemented the business-within-a-business organization – the struggles, the lessons, and the results of an organizational reinvention.

N. Dean Meyer's organizational design framework provided the map for our journey. His books provided the scientific grounding I had long searched for, and his support as a transformation consultant and executive coach helped crystallize the principles behind what we lived through.

Dean collaborated with me on the editorial structure of this book, especially in the chapters where I describe his methodology. His words appear alongside mine – but the story, the experience, and the lessons are uniquely ours.

This is not a manual about his method. It's a case study of what happens when those ideas are applied in the real world – imperfectly, courageously, and under the constant pressure of delivering results.

I didn't write this book to celebrate success. I wrote it as part of my own ongoing journey of refinement and learning. As we transformed PDC, I came to understand that real growth – personal and organizational – comes from reflecting, sharing, and supporting others navigating similar challenges.

My hope is that this book serves as educational material for our own people as we continue evolving together, and for others who might find these lessons useful in their own transformations.

As James Clear so wisely put it: "The teacher learns more than the student. The author learns more than the reader."

Writing this book has deepened my understanding of what we built at PDC – and what we have yet to build. I hope it contributes to your personal and organizational growth as well.

Foreword

by N. Dean Meyer
author and organizational transformation expert

Sergio Paiz did a brilliant job of turning around his company. This was, in part, because he's a brilliant business strategist. But, of course, it takes an organization to execute those strategies. Sergio understood this from the start, and his organizational transformation was a core element of his turn-around strategy.

He didn't just rescue a company. He built a showcase organization in the process. Now, PDC is a leading example of a company built on the principles of the business-within-a-business organization.

The results are remarkable. His team focuses on multiple products, markets, and geographies – all without building silos that undermine corporate synergies and performance.

Teamwork is the way they work. His leaders dynamically assemble talent from throughout the entire enterprise to address problems and opportunities – talent that brings depth of expertise in their specialties thanks to treating every function as a shared service.

And for every initiative or operational process, accountabilities are clear. There's a single group accountable for the whole, and every team member has clear individual accountabilities for sub-results.

Sergio integrates acquisitions with ease, delivering intended two-way synergies in months, not years.

Staff at all levels are highly engaged and loyal, in large part due to empowerment, opportunities for creativity and innovation, and a sense of purpose that comes from serving others (internal and external customers).

And there's an entrepreneurial spirit – what Sergio calls an ownership mentality – that permeates the entire leadership team.

Sergio kindly said that all this would not have been possible without my vision of an organization defined as a network of businesses within a business; principles of organizational design; and a change-management process designed to shift people's thinking from traditional forms to those of empowered internal entrepreneurs. But I assure you, it has been a two-way street! I learned so much working alongside him on this transformation.

On a personal note, in addition to his brilliance in both business strategy and organizational strategy, Sergio is a beautiful human being, exhibiting compassion, humility, wisdom, and a commitment to life-long learning. I'm awed by all he's accomplished, and honored to have been alongside him throughout this adventure.

Introduction

Every great story starts with a mission. For PDC, it was never just about building a profitable company – it was about transforming the lives of our people, the communities where we operate, and our customers, while creating a legacy that would endure for generations.

Today, PDC is a fully integrated, multi-business, multi-country leader in its industry, known for its innovative organizational model and its culture of entrepreneurship and empowerment. We've enjoyed double-digit growth, outstanding employee engagement, and a company that is resilient in the face of challenges.

But it wasn't always this way.

This book tells the story of how a struggling, broken distribution company – teetering on the brink of collapse – evolved into a thriving consumer products enterprise. It's a story about facing seemingly impossible challenges, making tough decisions, and taking the long view.

It's also a story about a radical organizational transformation, grounded in N. Dean Meyer's vision of a business-within-a-business model – a framework designed to build a high-performing, agile, and entrepreneurial company that can scale indefinitely.

Just as a winning sports team doesn't rely solely on individual talent, but on the right formations, playbooks, and relentless practice, so too in business. Success demands not just great people, but a well-designed organizational operating model that aligns everyone toward shared goals.

We approached our transformation much like a championship team: recruiting top talent, designing our "formations" (structure, culture, governance, and metrics), and perfecting our "plays" (teamwork, financial coordination, and planning processes) – all with the aim of building an empowered organization capable of extraordinary results.

Before I tell you how we did it, let me show you who we are today.

As of this writing, PDC generates nearly half a billion dollars in annual revenues through a number of distinct businesses, including:

- Home care products
- Dairy products
- Food products
- Personal Care Products
- Distribution services
- Software services
- HR services
- Promotional services
- Digital marketing services

PDC operates across several countries, serving diverse markets as one fully integrated company.

We've grown through eight acquisitions to date – not only acquiring businesses, but integrating them quickly and seamlessly into our organizational operating model, transforming each one into a thriving part of our ecosystem.

Since the transformation began 15 years ago, our profitability has increased 29-fold, and we have every reason to believe that our track record of 30% per year growth in EBITDA (earnings) will continue.

More importantly, our people are thriving. We've built an ecosystem where everyone has a stake in the company's success and knows their role in driving it. We're proud to be widely recognized as a great place to work.

We enjoy high levels of engagement and satisfaction. Today, our 3,000 associates report an 88% happiness index, measured rigorously every six months. This metric is more than just a number – it reflects our commitment to creating an environment where employees feel valued, empowered, and fulfilled.

We credit this success to our unique organizational design. Though we have a traditional hierarchy on paper, we operate as a network of entrepreneurial businesses. Every team is accountable and focused on delivering extraordinary results to its customers – whether external or internal.

Our leaders run their areas like business owners – empowered to make decisions, innovate, and deliver outcomes. This culture of ownership has transformed not just our operations, but our people.

At the heart of this transformation is SIGO – Sistema Integral de Gestión Organizacional (Integrated Organizational Management System). SIGO is not a single methodology, but a fully integrated Business Operating System, built from over 46 systems we've adopted and tailored over time – including tools for strategy, financial discipline, talent development, culture, and execution.

Beneath all these lies a foundational layer: our organizational design. This defines how we are structured, how work gets done (team formations), how we behave as internal entrepreneurs (culture), and how we measure success (our internal economy). Without this layer, SIGO would be fragmented – a collection of disconnected tools without cohesion.

Dean Meyer's organizational design principles and frameworks became the cornerstone of everything we've built. This book describes how we implemented Dean's model at PDC – and how it allowed us to scale rapidly and sustainably.

(The "Designed to Scale" component of the SIGO model represents this foundational layer.)

While SIGO also includes three other components – People First, Strategy and Execution, and Financial Discipline – this book focuses specifically on organizational design, the system that makes all others work in harmony.

This book is a case study of our organizational design journey, and how it enabled the transformation of PDC.

1. A Bit of Personal History First

My path from engineer and entrepreneur to CEO of a fairly significant company (at least by Central American standards) was born from a sad and consequential event. Here's my personal story....

The Family Business

Our family business was founded by my grandfather, Carlos. He was an orphan, and came from very humble beginnings. He traveled daily to the market to sell fruit to earn a meager living. But eventually, he became a very successful self-made entrepreneur.

With the help of his children (my father and uncles), they created what became Central America's largest retail company. It included the leading chain of grocery stores in Central America (Paiz stores), as well as an extensive sales and distribution network.

I learned many things from my grandfather. For one, he taught us to be entrepreneurs from a very early age. I built my first business renting Nintendo games at age 8. My second venture, which started at age 15, produced and sold plastic pitchers for milk.

But the most important lesson my grandfather taught me was that "being good is good business." He always remained rooted in his humble beginnings; and he always looked out for his employees. For example, he created the first Equity and Profit-Sharing program in Central America.

(My brother, Salvador, with our grandfather, Carlos, drafting a new venture agreement.)

My First Venture

After graduating from Lehigh University in Pennsylvania, I got a job as an engineer in a logistics consulting company. They sent me to several countries to help design logistics networks for several clients.

After two years, and in the middle of the dot-com bonanza, I decided to quit my job and start a technology venture with my brother, Salvador. We developed business software – initially for our family business – including a Warehouse Management System and a Sales Force Automation System, on early hand-held "personal digital assistant" (PDA) devices.

We had several technology challenges back then, like the inability of those early platforms to scale reliably and cost effectively. However, the software worked well, and we started to expand to other customers in the region.

These entrepreneurial beginnings developed in me an outlook on business that became the foundation of my leadership style and organizational vision. We'll come to that a bit later....

The Beginning of the End of Our Tech Venture

As our software business grew, my father started to get anxious. He was having difficulties in several of the businesses the family was involved in. And he was getting tired. He was proud of our entrepreneurial spirit; but he was looking for his sons to step in and help him out. So, he was not happy that we were venturing out on our own.

My father was a man of few words. One evening, he invited me for dinner, where he not-too-subtly hinted that my "hobby" was going nowhere, and that I should consider working with him full time.

He did, however, encourage me to first get my MBA abroad before I came back to work in the family business.

At that time, our software business was still in the start-up phase. Employees we had just hired were depending on us. Customers that I personally had sold were counting on the software running reliably, and we still had a long way to go in terms of quality and functionality. Leaving the company didn't seem appropriate at the time.

But I was feeling bad about not helping my dad. I was torn. After a lot of reflection, in 2001, I dutifully sent in applications to several US business schools. I felt reasonably confident that I'd be accepted by at least one of them, and started to look forward to it. I never imagined I wouldn't get the chance to attend.

Tragedy

On September 11, 2002, the feeling at the office was gloomy, as it was the one-year anniversary of 9/11. I was 26 years old.

My phone rang. The news was devastating. Father's plane was missing.

That morning, my father had flown on a philanthropic mission to El Salvador with other regional business executives. His plane never arrived.

I immediately drove to the airport, as did Salvador. We started to arrange transportation; but a rescue mission was already prepared to go. My brother and I were able to hop in the rescue helicopter.

The news was not good.

Family Challenges

The same year that my father died, our Dutch partner, Royal Ahold, got into legal problems in the US for its questionable accounting practices. Their US public stock plummeted as a result of this scandal, which forced them to divest several operations globally, including their minority stake in our family's company.

There were many different views in the extended family about whom we'd authorize to acquire Ahold's shares. It was a stressful time for all of us.

After a few difficult years, in 2005, Walmart acquired our grocery business.

My branch of the Paiz family, Paiz del Carmen (PDC), took over the distribution business and a financial services company that remained. My brother, Salvador, took on the financial services business, while I led the distribution company as chairman of its Board.

From my Board perspective, I observed serious problems in the distribution business. It was deteriorating quickly. Time was running out.

2. What I Inherited

When I first agreed (with my family) to accept responsibility for the distribution business, I had no idea of the challenges I was taking on....

The Distribution Business

Most major brands in Latin America used 3rd party distributors like ours to get their products into the retail channels, to ensure that consumers' needs are met, and to build the brand's exposure in the market. Distributors have large sales forces that develop relationships with shop owners of all sizes, from big retail chains to small "mom-and-pop" neighborhood stores commonly known as "tienditas."

The Paiz distribution business, called Codisa, had exclusive distribution rights in Guatemala for more than 21 commercial partners, representing more than 80 well-known brands, including Essity, SC Johnson, Hershey's, Otis McAllister, Pringles, and L'Oréal.

In Guatemala, a country of 16 million people, there are around 110,000 tienditas, of which PDC had direct relationships with approximately 55%. We also sold partners' consumer goods through larger retailers, including Walmart.

I learned quickly that distribution is not an easy business. We had to visit and deliver nationwide to 60,000 customers per week, with an average ticket of just $10. Typical margins for a distributor of consumer products are between 19 and 22%. Low margins, plus complex operations, make the industry unattractive to investors.

The Mess

Codisa was well established. However, it was generating heavy losses. And there was no growth strategy.

The more I learned, the worse things appeared. Our culture was fractured, and morale had hit an all-time low. I discovered a lot of internal fraud, including at the executive level. I found that inventory was being stolen from the main warehouse. I learned that we had an organized crime unit operating inside our warehouse, led by a local gang member. Things were getting dangerous.

Execution was faltering, and our overall performance was poor. It came as little surprise when we lost the Essity contract, a major Swedish personal care company and one of our largest partnerships. The loss of this business further exacerbated our already weakened financial position.

And we had incurred significant debt. In truth, Codisa was on the verge of bankruptcy.

Our banks were getting nervous now that my father was gone. They were calling me literally every week, and their demands and threats intensified. I went to bed each night dreading the morning light, because I knew it meant another day of overwhelming operational problems and aggressive calls from the banks.

I remember getting home after work each day feeling utterly exhausted. At night, I would stare at the ceiling for hours, pondering how to repay the banks. How to fix the business. How to fix the culture.

Frankly, I had no idea what I was doing. I had no business experience, no leadership experience, and no finance experience. I didn't know where to start. I felt insecure and extremely anxious, even to the point of feeling nauseous going into the office on some days.

We tried four different CEOs. None could solve our complex problems.

I worked intensely, non-stop. But working hard was not the solution. I was failing miserably. After two years of my leadership of the Board, the company was worse off, losing even more money and in a downward spiral.

I found myself presiding over an existential crisis.

Einstein's Advice on Crises

The following quote about crises is commonly attributed to Albert Einstein in a 1931 letter to *The Crisis* magazine (though this is not verified):

> *"Crisis is the best blessing that can happen to people and countries, because crisis brings progress. Creativity arises from distress as the day springs from the dark night. It is in crisis that inventiveness, discoveries, and great strategies are born. Those who overcome a crisis overcome themselves without being overcome.*
>
> *"Those who attribute their failures and hardships to the crisis violate their own talent, and respect problems more than solutions. The true crisis is the crisis of incompetence. The problem with people and countries is the laziness to find solutions.*
>
> *"To speak of crisis is to promote it, and to remain silent in crisis is to extol conformism. Instead, let us work hard. Let's once and for all end the only threatening crisis, which is the tragedy of not wanting to fight to overcome it."*
>
> *- Albert Einstein*

With that advice, perhaps I should have been feeling positive about the mess. Realistically, there was nowhere to go but up!

Life-long Learning

But the crisis was taking its toll. One day, I woke up with a pain in my chest and ended up in the hospital. I was physically and emotionally burned out.

My doctor told me, "Sergio, you need to slow down. You need to change your lifestyle." He gave me a book about a morning routine which forever changed my life.

Each morning, I woke up early and dedicated time to inner growth and reflection – not only intellectual growth, but also emotional and spiritual growth. As Warren Buffet would later say, "...the best protection against inflation is investing in your own skills."

Many corporate leaders just maintain (or marginally improve) the performance of their organizations, often based on their intuition and experience, but not on study.

Their attitude toward learning was not for me. As an entrepreneur, good is never good enough. And with regard to my own skills, I couldn't be complacent. I couldn't stop learning.

> "Men give me some credit for genius.
>
> "All the genius I have lies in this:
>
> "When I have a subject in hand, I study it profoundly. Day and night it is before me. I explore it in all its bearings. My mind becomes pervaded with it.
>
> "Then the efforts that I make are what people are pleased to call the fruits of genius. It is the fruit of labor and thought."
>
> - Alexander Hamilton -

How does one go about learning? Charlie Munger said:

> *"I believe in the discipline of mastering the best of what other people have figured out. I don't believe in just sitting down and trying to dream it up all yourself. Nobody's that smart."*
>
> *- Charlie Munger*

Somewhere else, I read that you can get brilliant knowledge from people who have devoted their life to a topic for less than a penny a page. Why would anyone pass up that opportunity!?

I read and reread books, then summarized them. I developed a passion for knowledge.

(I still believe that life-long learning is a critical trait of leadership. This is the kind of attitude I want in all our leaders. I believe the most valuable employees are not the ones who know the most, but the ones that are able to learn the fastest. Or as Dr. Seuss [1] wrote, "It's better to know how to learn than to know.")

Learning about Finance

Clearly, our financial crisis was the most pressing. If only I'd had the benefit of an MBA....

As I started to read about finance, I discovered that it is not as difficult as I had feared.

We've all heard that the fastest way to learn is to teach. As the saying goes, "I see and I forget; I read and I remember; I teach and I understand."

So, one day, I got this crazy idea. I went to our local university and asked if there were any opportunities to teach finance. To my surprise, they gave me a position teaching corporate finance, which I continued to do for over a decade.

That foot in both worlds (business and academia) has been beneficial for me. As Dave Snowden said: [2]

> *"It is a truth that should be universally acknowledged, that the majority of those who use the word 'academic' in a pejorative or dismissive way are simply trying to find a convenient excuse for their own lack of knowledge and/or willingness to study something before practice.*
>
> *"Without theory, practice is questionable and doesn't scale. Without practice, theory does not develop. Creating a dichotomy between the two is inauthentic at best, duplicitous at worst."*

- David Snowden

Yes, each augments the other.

Ultimately, I became proficient in finance. And I practiced what I'd learned in the company.

Now (years later) I have been invited to participate on other companies' Boards. In one, I'm leading the Finance Committee and teaching the CFO best practices in financial accounting, tax optimization, etc. The other Board is in a bank, where I was chosen to lead the Credit Committee that approves all credit deals above a certain amount. Looking back, I find it amusing that I ended up leading these teams with no formal financial education. I guess this was validation of the fruits of diligent study.

Learning about Leadership

After studying finance, I began reading about leading people, performance management, compensation, and so on. Of course, this is every bit as important as finance.

I also read many books about other companies, getting a sense of what works and what doesn't. It was a constant quest to understand what makes a great company.

Learning about Organizations

I really enjoyed my mornings of learning and growth. My intense quest for knowledge was in large part fueled by my desire to fix our company at its core – its fundamental organizational operating model.

I have always been inspired by excellence. I admired those rare global organizations that operated with excellence; and I dreamed of a transformation that would take us to this level. By "this level," I mean an organizational operating model that would be autonomous and self-evolving, one that continually innovates, self-adjusts, and self-develops. And one that delivers great results for both its customers and its staff.

Surely there must be great books written on that.

I had read many good leadership books and biographies, but none really delved into the science of how to design a high-performing organization.

I queried Amazon every day, skimming through several books on organizational design. But all were the same: superficial, with shallow quick-fix advice. Many just focused on Human Resources issues. Most described organizational design as an art, the product of the style and preferences of the CEO. None offered a scientific approach.

It was frustrating. Why is this so complex; and why is there so little literature out there on this subject?

One day, as I fine-tuned my searches on Amazon, a little blue book by N. Dean Meyer came up, called *The Building Blocks of Structure*. As soon as I started to read it, I was hooked. This was the science I'd been seeking.

> (That book has since been superseded by an even more comprehensive book, *Principle-based Organizational Structure*. [3] And Dean's work is best understood by starting with his capstone book, *How Organizations Should Work*. [4])

I read the whole book, re-read it, summarized it, and then bought other books by Dean.

> "The game of life is the game of everlasting learning. At least it is if you want to win."
>
> - Charlie Munger -

What I found both unique and very appealing about Dean's work was (and is) this: He offers a scientific approach to organizational systems such as structure, culture, metrics, and resource-governance processes. And his work adds up to a comprehensive approach to organizational design (far beyond just organization charts).

I thought to myself, it would be really great if I could talk with the author. But I worried that this famous author would never reply to a guy in Guatemala who is leading this little broken company.

I wrote to Dean anyway. To my surprise, he replied. He has been helping me ever since, as a coach and friend, as well as our transformation consultant.

3. What I Did: The Triage Phase

We had big problems, and we needed solutions right away! I had to put my learnings into action.

Leadership and Legal Control

I knew that I couldn't fix the problems from a Board position. I'd need to take on an operational role to drive real changes.

But I had no leadership experience. I was shy, introverted, and terrified of speaking in public. In addition, I felt really insecure about my lack of formal education, given that most people who would report to me had MBAs.

Nonetheless, I really had no choice. The four CEO's that we'd hired had failed to turn the company around. Ultimately, I stepped up (technically, down from chair of the Board) to the role of CEO of Codisa.

In 2011, I accepted. The day of the transition was a disaster. The old CEO gave a magnificent departing speech, and then I was invited as the new CEO to take the stage in front of 500 people. I froze. I couldn't speak. After taking a deep breath, I then gave a timid speech with terrible content.

I felt so embarrassed that, when I got home that night... well, you can anticipate what I did. I immediately started searching for public speaking books and courses. I chose a local course by Dale Carnegie. This one-month course cost $500, and was a really great investment.

I struggled during my first year on the job. But with the benefit of studying Dean's work and seeking his counsel, I began to see the root causes of the company's serious problems.

Two big challenges popped out: I saw key weaknesses in the organizational structure. And obviously, the culture was seriously broken.

Knowing significant changes were required, I needed complete control of the organization. We had other investors with seats on my Board. They did not share my vision of building a great organization, perhaps because it would require a significant investment in transformation.

In 2011, we were able to buy them all out, and with my brother and sister, took sole legal control. After that, I started making needed changes. This was the beginning of the transformation of Codisa into Grupo PDC ("PDC").

Triage List

There are two kinds of changes I could make: I could address the symptoms, and I could address root causes.

I wanted to address root causes, but some problems were so urgent that I had no choice but to fix them directly. I put these on a "triage" list. I had to get these out of the way before I could embark on a real organizational transformation.

Quick Fixes 1: Urgent People Decisions

Early on, I was forced to replace key members of the leadership team.

We had serious ethics problems throughout the organization. In one case, a top executive had their wife on the payroll as a contractor, with no apparent deliverables. Another executive had been falsifying the books to achieve his metrics, and we believe he'd been embezzling money.

There is no room in our organization for anything less than impeccable ethics.

Beyond these extreme cases, there was a general lack of accountability, empowerment, initiative, creativity, drive – all the things we desperately needed from our talent.

Overall, I fired over 40 managers in those first two years (including half of the senior leadership team). This took an emotional toll on me. Even though I knew these people were harming the organization and the rest of our staff, the process of firing them was extremely painful. Some were very confrontational and vocal; others just acknowledged their wrong-doing and left.

Firing all these people was just half of the challenge. Obviously, I then had the problem of hiring 40 new leaders. I started to search for executives in successful multinational firms, thinking they would bring the experience we needed and I lacked. However, most of them weren't willing to talk to us. They had stable jobs in top firms, and would not risk their careers going to a bankrupt company with a broken culture. (There was a lot of noise in the market about our crisis.)

I had lengthy meetings with candidates over coffee. I told them about our vision of becoming a company that cared for people and that had the purpose of transforming lives. I also created an equity package, and invited them to be my partners in this transformation journey we were about to embark on.

The equity package helped us get candidates' attention. Ultimately, we were able to fill all 40 positions with great people who were motivated by the vision.

Quick Fixes 2: People First

With the new leadership team, we developed a set of values that put our employees first.

Those values led us to revitalize employee benefits. But benefits alone don't change a culture.

> "Your employees come first. If you treat them well, then they treat the customers well, and that means your customers come back and your shareholders are happy."
>
> - Herb Kelleher -
> Founder, Southwest Airlines

We implemented open offices, even for executives, leading to much more visibility of, and interaction with, the leaders in our organization. My objective was an open and transparent environment.

Managers could not believe I was tearing down their offices, which were a status symbol. I think it helped that I led by example, not having an office myself.

I would work at any available desk in the open office. At first, staff were afraid to sit next to me. But after a while, they understood that I was accessible to everyone. This is not common in a country where leaders generally do not interact directly with operating staff.

For me, it was fun. I see myself as a servant leader, where my job is to understand everyone's problems and then find a way to make their lives easier and better (and improve their performance in the process). I enjoyed saying hello to anyone who sat next to me, and I asked them how their day was going. I would get incredible insights into their jobs and our pressing challenges just by having these short conversations.

Initially, servant leadership was hard for our senior leaders to grasp. I would constantly remind them that we were at the base of the "inverted pyramid"; and our operating team – the people who were creating value day-to-day – were at the top. I drove home that our role as leaders was to figure out how to help them succeed. In the end, if our staff were successful, we would all be successful.

> "The first responsibility of a leader is to define responsibilities. The last is to say thank you. In between, the leader is a servant."
>
> - Max De Pree -

Of course, our executives ultimately came to understand – and now, sincerely value – servant leadership.

The culture throughout the company started to shift. People started to talk to each other, rather than sending emails from one closed office to another. We would team up quickly, on the spot, to resolve burning issues. Great things started to happen.

Quick Fixes 3: Technologies and Processes

We also invested in introducing new technologies and processes to solve inefficiencies.

We implemented a modern ERP solution, and started to get our financials and operations in order. We also implemented a salesforce automation solution, and the warehouse management system from my old software start-up.

It wasn't just technology for technology's sake, but technology that could help us improve our operations. We re-engineered processes in the course of implementing these new systems, and configured the systems to support the new processes.

We also introduced performance practices such as a daily huddle of all the people involved in key value-chain teams (order-to-cash for supermarkets, for example). In these 10-minute standing-up meetings, people present their last day's performance results, and develop plans for the week to improve performance.

We measure performance through Value Stream Maps (a Lean methodology). For example, we measure the prior day's process time and wait time for all processes within our value chains. We use technology to capture these value streams in real time, and we display the statistics on a huge screen in an open office. Visitors who tour our facilities often take pictures of this.

We Needed *Transformation*

These people/technology/process changes improved things, each solving specific problems. But taken together, they were not enough. Every time I solved one problem, another cropped up. I didn't want to spend my life playing "Whack-a-Mole" ®

Most leadership books state that hiring the best people is key. But bringing in some great people at every level wasn't enough either.

Great people are great; but they can't overcome a bad organization. We needed more than great people, processes, and technologies. We needed a fundamental transformation in the organization to address the root causes of our problems.

> "Great people in a bad organizational ecosystem will fail.
>
> "And a normal bell-curve of people in a well-designed organization can succeed."
>
> \- N. Dean Meyer -

And with that realization, I had no choice but to commit to rethinking every aspect of our organizational design – a real transformation.

> "Continuous improvement isn't nearly as important as discontinuous improvement.... A creative act breaks with the chain that has come before it.
>
> "One never becomes a leader by continuously improving; that's imitation of a leader.... You only become a leader by leapfrogging those who are ahead of you. And that comes about through creativity."
>
> \- Dr. Russell Ackoff [5] -

4. Transformation To What?

Knowing that big changes were needed – fundamental changes in the way the company works – it was tempting to jump in and start planning a change process. But that's just the mechanics of transformation.

It's clear that one can use those mechanics to build any kind of organization, good or bad. As the old saying goes, "If you don't know where you're going, any road will do."

Before I started changing things, I needed to define the end-state – a blueprint (like a high-level engineering drawing) of the future organization that we were about to build. This would help us ensure that every change we'd make along our transformation journey would add up to a consistent end-state, without zig-zagging along that path.

Dean proposes two "Pillars" of that organizational vision: the business-within-a-business paradigm, and empowerment. All other principles are at a minimum compatible with, and many are actually derived from, these two.

These core principles guide every decision we make, from how we structure teams to how we approach customer relationships.

Pillar One: The Business-within-a-business Paradigm

Personally, I am very entrepreneurial. I was (and am) enthusiastic about extending that spirit down to everyone in the company. I wanted everyone, at every level, to think and act like a business owner.

How Owners Think

Many other companies have implemented "shared services" – support functions that serve the rest of the company. But they have not necessarily implemented the owner mentality.

Consider this: How often do you wash a rental car? What quality of fuel do you choose for a rental vehicle? Do you look into that ticking sound coming from the engine? Now, compare these behaviors with how you maintain your own car.

This contrast illustrates the profound difference in attitude between using things that are not yours and true ownership – between an employee and a business owner.

What Owners Do

Beyond just caring, what is it that owners do for their businesses?

Consider some of the things that entrepreneurs do to make their companies successful (Figure 1).

Figure 1: What Entrepreneurs Do [6]

- Build great partnerships with customers
- Proactively contribute to customers' strategies
- Offer a comprehensive, innovative catalog of services
- Offer best value
- Give customers control of what they buy
- Flexibly tailor solutions to customers' needs
- Meet every commitment
- Optimize the safety of the enterprise's assets (including information) and people
- Innovate in ways that prepare them to deliver tomorrow's opportunities

As an entrepreneur, I know I don't have a monopoly. I must earn my customers' business.

In order to ensure that we survive in competitive markets, we must constantly innovate, while also making sure the value proposition we deliver to our customers is right. We also must have impeccable delivery through operational excellence.

And we entrepreneurs must invest in having an incredible relationship with our customers. Here's an example....

I recently visited a company in Peru that provides manufacturing services for consumer products companies like ours. They serve many global brands. I was greeted by their CEO at the airport. He drove us to their manufacturing facilities, where he and his leaders gave a thorough presentation on their competencies. Afterwards, we toured their facilities. Then, he invited us to lunch. With all that attention from the CEO, it was clear to me that this was an entrepreneur who wanted our business.

These behaviors are exactly what we want from everyone in every corner of our organization, whether they serve external customers or others within the company. Why can't our internal manufacturing area behave like that CEO in Peru – the owner of a manufacturing services company serving our internal customers (the leaders who manage our brands)? Why can't *all* areas in the company be run like customer focused, entrepreneurial businesses within the business?

By "ownership thinking," I don't mean just that everybody cares about the success of the enterprise in the external market, though that of course is critical too. In thinking about the future of our company, I envisioned an environment where every leader (in every function, at every level) would nurture and care for their part of the business as if it were their own little company.

Ownership Thinking Isn't About Ownership

What does it take for employees to have this owners' motivation and drive, and to think and act like entrepreneurs?

Some people think that giving people a stake in the company will cause them to think like owners. But I've observed that ownership thinking has little to do with having shares of a company (or bonuses based on enterprise profits).

We did, in fact, implement an employee equity ownership program. But that was not what created an ownership mentality.

Note that there are companies that have equity ownership programs, like ESOPs, but don't have an entrepreneurial culture. In fact, recently, I met a member of the Board of the Association of ESOPs in the US. His greatest concern was that most of the ESOP companies in the Association did not have an ownership culture. Employees in these ESOP companies were actual owners, but they didn't think and act like owners!

So, "ownership thinking" must therefore be something that is intentionally built into the organization's design. As I'll describe below, we implemented an ownership culture long before we introduced our equity ownership program.

The Key to Ownership Thinking: Purpose

Over the years, I've observed many owners; and I've used my own experiences as an entrepreneur and owner to try to understand their motivations. What drives them?

It all seems to come down to this: Entrepreneurs are energized by having a grand challenge – a *purpose*. They are passionate about taking on big goals and delivering real value to customers and society. They are motivated to leave a legacy. They see their work as a grand piece of art.

PDC has a strong sense of purpose; but that's at the enterprise level. Building on that, I wanted every little group to have its own sense of purpose and value to others.

> "Purpose: using one's unique talents to do something hard (something to be proud of)
> that is of real value to others."
>
> - N. Dean Meyer [7] -

I could easily see how internal entrepreneurship would do that. Everybody would see that their work (their products and services) benefits others, typically people they know within the company. And this sense of purpose would both enhance everybody's performance and make us a great place to work.

Implementing Ownership Thinking

The business-within-a-business paradigm is designed into our organization chart. Every box on the organization chart is defined as a line of business, whether its customers are external or internal.

It's defined not by roles in processes, responsibilities for tasks, or staff's competencies. Every box on the organization chart is defined by what it "sells." (I'm not talking about money changing hands, i.e., internal transfer pricing. It's just a way to think about one's job.)

We stress that people get budgets not to pay their costs, but to provide their products and services to customers, both externally and within the company.

But we do not charge one another for services ("charge-backs," or transfer pricing). Actual internal money transfers are not necessary to implement ownership thinking; and they create an administrative burden and unnecessary risks. One risk is that charge-backs encourage internal customers to take their business outside instead of working through internal suppliers which are struggling to improve their competitive position. This can lead to fragmentation and lost enterprise synergies, and a loss of scale (and ultimately a loss of capabilities) in some internal lines of business. We work through one another, not around one another. We help our internal suppliers succeed (perhaps by utilizing those same external suppliers as extensions to their staff). We have no need for charge-backs.

Role of Managers

We understand that bosses are not staff's customers. Their real customers are people throughout the enterprise (and beyond) who benefit from their work. Pleasing those customers will, of course, please their bosses.

A boss is responsible for the performance review of an individual. Customers (internal or external) provide input to their performance appraisals.

But bosses look beyond just successful delivery of projects and services. Leaders of these businesses-within-the-business are accountable not just for the delivery of today's projects and services with excellence. They are also responsible for running a business, making sure it's cost-competitive, and innovating to remain competitive in the future.

Role of Hierarchy

Our organization is still a hierarchy, such as you see on any organization chart. The hierarchy sorts out all our internal lines of business, with no gaps and no overlaps. And the management structure is useful for talent management (hire, inspire), and for communications and coordination at the level of policies and strategies. Bosses are also accountable for mentoring their staff.

But the hierarchy is not for command and control. Our organization chart houses a network of internal entrepreneurships that serve each other – across multiple countries and multiple product lines. We share a common vision and purpose. And yet every function, being customer focused, tailors its products and services to the needs of its internal customers.

The end design is a network of businesses-within-a-business that work together in pursuit of the vision.

With this, we've instilled entrepreneurial thinking at the local group level. This ownership mindset is now deeply rooted at all levels of the organization, driving noticeable improvements in both engagement and performance.

I think this brings out the best in people. They become customer focused, results-oriented, frugal, and innovative. They team well because internal customer-supplier relationships clarify respective accountabilities (not the "one for all, all for one" mentality that leads people to meddle in others' domains of expertise and leaves no one accountable for results). We have widespread understanding of, and engagement in, the company's challenges and successes, but from the pragmatic perspective of what each of their groups can uniquely contribute.

Our structure also gives people a sense of purpose at the local level: creating value for others. They understand that they are, in fact, internal business owners.

Reinforcing Ownership Thinking

Building on our business-within-a-business organizational design, we later implemented an equity ownership program. This caused staff to become intensely interested in the success of the enterprise.

We then gave them a deep understanding of where corporate profits come from with the Great Game of Business (GGOB) methodology, becoming an open-book company that educates everyone on basic financial literacy, and then shares financial statements monthly with all employees.

Additionally, we implemented a forward-forecasting system where each of our 160 leaders is responsible for a specific line-item in the financial statements (their internal businesses' financial impacts). This allows us to forecast our month-end results in less than 20 minutes per week, and quickly launch gap-closing initiatives when necessary.

While ownership thinking was already in place thanks to the organizational design, the addition of actual ownership (our equity ownership program) and an understanding of where profits come from (GGOB and forward forecasting) combined to create a powerful synergy, and sparked a tremendous increase in commitment and engagement. The results have been nothing short of astounding for both the company and our leadership team, as I'll describe below.

Pillar Two: Empowerment

Dean's second Pillar is "empowerment."

This resonated with me. As an entrepreneur, I love the empowerment that comes with owning a business... the freedom to work whenever and wherever I want, do things my own way, and determine the future of my business.

Entrepreneurs know they are fully accountable for the success of their businesses. They want the authorities to go with that accountability.

This, in fact, is the very definition of empowerment: *One's authorities match one's accountabilities.* [8]

Empowerment creates engagement. And engagement drives performance. Consider the research findings on the impacts of highly engaged teams, as compared to lower engagement levels, in Figure 2.

Figure 2: The Impacts of Employee Engagement

- **Profits**: 23% higher [9]
- **Sales**: 18% higher [10]
- **Customer loyalty/engagement**: 10% higher [11]
- **Productivity**: 14-21% higher [12]
- **Quality problems (defects)**: 41% lower [13]
- **Shrinkage (theft)**: 28% lower [14]
- **Safety incidents (accidents)**: 64% lower [15]
- **Employee turnover**: 43% lower in low-turnover organizations, 18% lower in high-turnover organizations [16]
- **Absenteeism**: 78-81% lower [17]

These statistics are validated by multiple other research studies. [18]

They demonstrate that engaged employees have substantial positive effects on organizational performance. And these statistics don't even capture the possibilities that are generated by the creativity and innovation that all our talent can offer.

Why wouldn't we invest in empowerment at every level in our company!?

Jim Collins, author of the book, *Good to Great*, coined a catchy phrase that describes the opposite of empowerment, and sadly describes many entrepreneurs: he called them "a genius with a thousand helpers." [19]

I've met successful entrepreneurs who embody this egocentric model.

They build magnificent businesses. But everything revolves around them. By necessity, they have a tight rein on every little aspect of the business. They plan, they purchase inventory, they invest in marketing, they sign the checks.... And to do all this, they're surrounded by a lot of obedient assistants, none of whom are empowered to run their pieces of the business.

These executives struggle to empower their next-tier leaders, perhaps for lack of vision, confidence, and an organizational design that coordinates people and ensures accountability for results without the need for micromanagement.

Clearly, the egocentric model has severe limitations with regard to scaling and succession.

As to scaling, that genius entrepreneur will be able to run their organization as long as their energy permits, and as long as the business doesn't get too large or complex for one person to manage. But eventually, adding more scale will add more complexity, until it becomes impossible for any human being to be on top of everything going on in every corner of the firm. At that point, the company may continue to run with minimal capacity for growth; or, it may grow and start to fail.

As to succession, when that entrepreneur leaves, there is no internal successor. No one has had experience leading, because nobody was empowered to do anything other than follow orders. At this stage, the entrepreneur typically has no choice but to sell the business.

This is not what The Tugboat Institute would call "evergreen" – a company that delivers long-term sustainable growth and positive impacts. [20]

Even if the challenges of scalability and succession are not yet critical, consider all the talent that's wasted by an egocentric leader – bright, creative people who could be contributing so much more. That alone limits an organization's success.

I have seen the unfortunate effects of this egocentric organizational operating model especially vividly when we acquired companies. When the previous owner left, the remaining team was left in confusion. They were accustomed to a boss who made all the decisions, and they just did as they were told (*management by activities*).

When they were confronted with our culture of empowerment (*management by results*), where they have both authorities and accountabilities and are expected to think and act like owners, most didn't know what to do. Some were able to grasp the opportunity and remain with us to have successful careers, while others were not self-starters and simply couldn't operate in this fashion and left.

For a business to be scalable and sustainable, and to tap all the talent in the organization to the fullest, its leaders must be empowered to run their respective pieces of the business. And the executive at the top must get out of doing other people's jobs for them (and micro-managing them), and rise up to a more strategic level.

Dean considers this second Pillar, empowerment, to be so fundamental to organizational performance that he calls it the "Golden Rule" of organizational design. He points out that separating authority and accountability cannot work. The person with authority (and not matching accountabilities) is unconstrained, and can issue orders without regard for the consequences. Meanwhile, the person with accountability (and insufficient authorities) can't get the job done, and often gets blamed for decisions made by the one with authority.

In other words, a person with authority and no accountability becomes a "tyrant" with no checks and balances; and the person with accountability and no authority becomes a helpless "victim" and "scapegoat" for mistakes made by the person with authority.

We could not allow this within our organization.

Pillar 1 (business-within-a-business) helped me see how we could accomplish Pillar 2 (empowerment). Effective customer-supplier relationships recognize customers' right to choose what they buy, while respecting suppliers' right to manage how they make it.

A clear example of this is when you go to a restaurant. As a customer, you have the right to purchase whatever you want from the menu, and you expect to receive a specific deliverable with quality (what you ordered, delivered hot and in a timely fashion). But you can't go to the kitchen and micromanage the cooks, telling them what ingredients to add or how to go about the preparation process.

The same should be true within a company. We ask one another for a final product or service (a result), but do not attempt to control all the activities of our internal suppliers that go into producing this deliverable.

Everybody is accountable for (internal) customer satisfaction, competitive costs, innovative products and services, and every other aspect of the success of their businesses within the business. And with those accountabilities come matching authorities. While their customers decide what they'll buy, internal entrepreneurs are empowered to run their businesses their way.

I was convinced we needed to match authorities with accountabilities and empower people throughout our organization. Too much depended on me. We had to make a shift to an organization where people make decisions within their domains, but without any loss of coordination and control.

I could see how this is critical to both enterprise success and employee engagement (as well as my own quality of life).

I later learned that these two Pillars would guide the design of our structure, culture, metrics, and more.

5. The Challenge of Multi-business, Multi-country

The two Pillars led me to the breakthrough that I was looking for. I assure you, our organizational design is nothing like the traditional organizations I see in other multi-business, multi-country companies.

But before I describe our organizational design, consider the business challenges we must be capable of handling....

In 2013, I attended an executive course at the Harvard Business School called, "Leading a Global Enterprise." I never forgot how the professor, Dr. William W. George, started his first lecture: "The biggest challenge any CEO will have is to solve the multi-business, multi-country complexity."

I agree. Designing an organization that operates multiple lines of business in multiple countries is probably one of the most difficult, and impactful, challenges I've faced. And I fully appreciate the importance of getting this right. A bad design will substantially impair enterprise performance.

First, let's examine the challenge, and then some traditional approaches that I rejected. After that (in the next chapter), I'll explain our unique design which handles all these complexities while delivering global synergies and economies of scale.

Dimensions of the Cube

Operating a diversity of businesses in many countries requires managing multiple dimensions simultaneously:

- ➢ Businesses (product and services)
- ➢ Countries and geographies
- ➢ Sales channels (types of customers)
- ➢ Functions (professional specializations)
- ➢ Legal entities

Businesses (Products and Services)

In our case, we have several product lines (categories), including dairy, packaged food, home cleaning products, and industrial chemicals. Adding complexity, we have broken these lines of business into sub-categories. In dairy, for example, we subdivide the category into powdered milk, fluid milk, yogurt, and so forth. We must manage profitability (profit-and-loss statements, P&Ls) by category and the sub-categories within them.

Countries and Geographies

We currently operate in seven countries. And we plan to expand our geographic footprint continually over time. Each country sells different product lines, depending on local tastes, the competitive landscape, and other factors. We must also manage P&Ls per country. Each country is further broken down into territories, where we again need to manage sub-P&Ls.

Sales Channels (Types of Customers)

We have a variety of customers, ranging from Walmart down to mom-and-pop tienditas, with very different buying patterns. We have some customers who buy just one of our product lines, and some who buy many or all. We have customers who operate in just one country; but we also have customers that are global and make purchase decisions centrally. We need to understand P&Ls per sales channel. That's essential to understanding our "costs to serve" each type of customer.

Functions (Professional Specializations)

Of course, our organization includes all the typical functions: sales, marketing, engineering, manufacturing, logistics, customer service, and all the usual business services such as enterprise planning, IT, HR, finance, procurement, facilities, and administration.

While some of those capabilities are specific to a product category (e.g., manufacturing is quite different for milk versus cleaning products), all these functions are needed to support many or all categories, in all countries. And we need to ensure that all those functions are competitive in costs, delivery, and innovation.

Therefore, we must also manage internal P&Ls for each.

Legal Entities

Overlaying all this, we have established multiple legal entities for reasons of tax and regulatory compliance. We currently have 14 legal entities (sometimes several per country), all of which are legally required to produce a P&L and pay their respective taxes.

Country GMs

It's like a five-dimensional cube. And we need to see, and manage, P&Ls on each of those dimensions.

When confronted with all this complexity, many CEOs simply throw their hands in the air and say, this is too hard. They create autonomous business units, either by country or product-line.

In Latin America, we see many big companies that have established country General Managers (GMs), accountable for the P&L of all the product lines within their geographic boundaries. Somehow, for some executives, political borders automatically require separate autonomous business units, perhaps because of their geographic distance from corporate headquarters (even in this digital age where we routinely manage people who live far away), or perhaps because of differences in local markets.

If you follow this thinking to its logical conclusion, its absurdity becomes apparent. I would observe that regions within a country are sometimes further from one another (both geographically and culturally) than they are from a neighboring country. If the unique needs of a geography required independent business units, one could argue that we would need a GM for each geographic region within each country.

But let's just picture a General Manager per country. Of course, these Country GMs need to control their factors of production (authorities to match their accountabilities), so they build their local empires. Support functions are decentralized, reporting to those business units, ostensibly to give country leaders control.

As I thought about Country business units and the decentralization of most functions, I came to appreciate the importance of specialization. Specialists outperform generalists. Their estimates are better because they've done similar things before. They deliver results more reliably because they know how. They're faster because they don't have to climb the learning curve with each new project, and they utilize the best methods and tools. They produce higher quality because they're experts. And the pace of innovation improves because they keep up with their professions.

The value of specialization is something we all understand in our daily lives. For example, if we needed brain surgery, we would obviously choose an expert neurosurgeon versus a primary-care doctor who is a generalist in medicine.

Country GMs, with their independent business units, result in decentralization, which leads to loss of specialization (and hence of professional excellence) in every supporting function. Small groups of generalists scattered among business units cannot possibly perform as well as a consolidated group of specialists. For example, a few IT staff in each country cannot deliver excellence in all the critical functions of IT such as artificial intelligence, data analytics, cybersecurity, cloud infrastructure, and so on. As a result of decentralization, costs rise, reliable delivery and quality suffer, and innovation slows.

Costs also go up as the Country business units reinvent methods, processes, and tools, claiming that "in their country, things are different." Sales methods and strategies, marketing campaigns, accounting policies, HR policies, quality and safety practices, and more inevitably vary by country. Best practices in one country are not reliably adopted in others.

And when things go wrong, it's hard to figure out which practices are at fault.

I know this all too well. When I first became CEO of PDC, everything was highly decentralized, making it difficult to establish consistent standards across operations. While local managers were putting in their best efforts to oversee their regions, there were significant variations in how things were done. For instance, I remember feeling frustrated by the lack of uniformity in our warehouses – each one worked differently. How could we optimize our operations, and consistently learn and evolve over time?

My biggest concern was the inconsistency in our safety and quality protocols across different sites. Why couldn't we identify a "best practice" and apply it uniformly across the company? And as new ideas emerged, why did our country managers struggle to adapt and implement these changes consistently?

Beyond reduced professional excellence, enterprise synergies are lost.

We had decentralized Finance to the business units. As a result, from a corporate perspective, it was hard to get an enterprise view. Prior to our reorganization, when IT was decentralized to our two business units, we had two separate ERP systems. I couldn't even get a consolidated set of financial statements for the enterprise!

I saw that decentralizing Logistics fragmented inventories, which increased the need for safety stocks, driving up inventory carrying costs.

Decentralizing the Engineering function to the various business units not only reduces specialization and performance. You'll also pay for a lot of reinvention (for example packaging engineering being replicated for each business unit). You could end up with inconsistent, but functionally equivalent, products in different countries. And less product commonality leads to higher inventory carrying costs, more costly repairs, lost economies of scale, and reduced buying power with vendors.

The same goes for Marketing, where decentralization undermines brand synergies. And if anyone at the enterprise level is charged with coordinating brands globally, they're set up to be in conflict with Country GMs who (naturally) demand the authorities to go with their accountabilities.

As for Sales, independent country business units do a poor job of aligning global channel strategies, and a poor job of serving global customers with corporate-level buyers.

In every function that's decentralized to country business units, cross-boundary collaboration suffers and enterprise synergies are lost.

This is exactly what we learned when we acquired our dairy business. It operated in two countries, with a GM in each country. Things got so decentralized that even the brand logo differed between the countries. The product portfolio grew to be different in each country, as well as the formulations and manufacturing practices. (Since the acquisition, we have consolidated the portfolio and now benefit from consistent branding and standardized R&D and manufacturing practices.)

And with Country business units, as you grow into more and more countries, you gain no advantages of size – no economies of scale, no greater depth of specialization, and no synergies.

In reality, country borders only add a dimension of legal and fiscal (tax) accounting differences, which are easily taken care of by general counsel, government relations, and financial services functions. And there is no reason why a centralized organization cannot tailor its product mix and marketing to local markets (whether that's defined by country borders or other more relevant segmentation factors). Nowadays in the digital age, managing across borders is straightforward and far more effective.

I see no upside to autonomous country business units.

Product-line GMs

Other CEOs may break the company into global product-focused business units, with Country Managers under each. As with Country GMs, this establishes relatively autonomous business units, this time by product instead of geography.

Now, you'll have multiple organizations (one for each product category) working independently in each country. That, too, is complex and expensive. You cannot present a single face to customers who buy multiple products, and you're likely to miss sales synergies (up-selling a customer with additional product lines).

With this approach, whose job is it to spot opportunities for new product lines, which could require entirely new business units? Much of the innovation has to come from the enterprise CEO. While I love working at that level, I don't want to be the sole source of innovation or constrain the creativity of any of my staff.

And when you do see an opportunity to develop a new product line (either through acquisitions or organically), you need to set up an entire new business unit (in every country). That's slow and expensive.

Additionally, organizing autonomous business units by product-line has all the same serious flaws as Country GMs – the costs of decentralization and reduced specialization, lost synergies, and weak enterprise collaboration.

Corporate Controls

From an enterprise perspective, either approach is disjointed. It's as if the enterprise becomes a holding company with minimal synergies.

Then, when a crisis occurs (for example, a safety incident), enterprise executives discover that local practices are far from robust. The enterprise CEO or Board may step in and attempt to fix this by overlaying a "Corporate Shared Services" group whose purpose is, in part, to control and police these business-unit GMs and their staff. Corporate HR oversees country HR; Corporate Finance oversees country Finance; etc.

Of course, this doesn't address the costs of decentralization: replication, reduced specialization, and lost synergies. And it adds the costs of redundancies in key functional areas.

And with Corporate looking over their shoulders, the operating companies feel disempowered. (In fact, they're right; they *are* disempowered.) Trying to defend their autonomy (so that they have authorities to match their accountabilities), they cooperate with corporate staff at the minimum level they can get away with. Relationships become adversarial. The culture becomes political.

The Matrix

Some companies try to address these problems with a "matrix" structure. Here, they add a second dimension of executives: one by country, and one by product line. Or perhaps one by country, and the other by function. Or is it one by product line, and the other by function?

Already, you can see that a matrix structure is going to sacrifice coordination on one dimension or another.

In a matrix organization, people have two bosses. This is terribly confusing for staff. Whom should they really listen to when there are conflicts in priorities and directions?

Bureaucratic processes are set up to align priorities and directions, where the multiple bosses negotiate and compete. This makes the company less agile.

And from what I've seen, these companies become highly political, with power rooted in personal relationships and skills of influence, rather than job performance.

Furthermore, as staff try to please two bosses, with little empowerment of their own, they learn that it's best to just follow orders. As a result, engagement and innovation are diminished.

"Before joining PDC, I worked in a matrix structure with two or more bosses, each of whom defined their priorities and focuses (normally not aligned with each other). It was hard on me, and ultimately it didn't work!

"At PDC, we are empowered; and priorities are clear (generally set by our internal customers). It's a high-performing organization, and a really great place to work!"

- Pedro Luis Marroquin -
Engineering Lead, PDC

The Organization du Jour

Many companies are so confused by all of this that they end up restructuring frequently. They lack coordination for in-country activities, so they decentralize to Country GMs. As a result, performance problems arise; and enterprise synergies aren't happening. Perhaps of greatest concern, product lines become fragmented.

Then, they shift to Product-focused business units. With that, they encounter the converse problem. They lose accountability for country results.

And they still lack focus on enterprise strategies. So, they overlay a controlling corporate staff or a matrix. That works poorly, so they centralize everything and both countries and product lines don't get the support they need.

And when that doesn't work, it's back to Country GMs!

Normally, it seems to take about five years to get the new approach working as best it can, only to find that while fixing one problem, they created many more. And with that discovery, the next restructuring is around the corner.

Each restructuring rips out the culture. People get frustrated and tired of trying to figure out how to get things done after each reorganization. They become cynical, morale degrades, and employee turnover increases. Disengaged employees and a damaged, convoluted, or ill-defined organizational operating model creates an organization that is inefficient, inconsistent, political, bureaucratic, and simply performs poorly. In the end, value is destroyed.

This "organization du jour" and the costly chaos it creates will go on forever, if you let it.

It doesn't matter how you cut it. Structuring autonomous business units around any one of the dimensions of the cube is far from satisfactory. Scale, efficiency, innovation, and enterprise synergies are all sacrificed in the name of simplicity.

But autonomous business units are not really simple at all. The challenge of the five dimensions doesn't go away. Autonomous business units just force the management of complexity (i.e., the coordination of all the various dimensions of the cube) one level down, leaving business unit leaders to manage it instead of the CEO.

I was certain I didn't want any of these models, despite how popular they are in other multi-business, multi-country companies. I was convinced we needed a breakthrough – a much more innovative and capable approach to organizational design.

6. Our Design: A Fully Integrated Company

We decided to address our multi-business, multi-country complexity with a very different approach. We do not have siloed business units with General Managers for each country or each product line. We are a *fully integrated company.*

I recently read an interesting article titled "Company of One" which takes this concept to the extreme, but makes the point. It envisions a central architect of a business – essentially a brand manager – who outsources every support requirement to world-class companies (sales, marketing, logistics, manufacturing, finance, human resources, etc.).

Of course, that means paying other shareholders their profits. Innovations in all those functions (other than brand-management itself) belong to others. Collaboration among the functions becomes purely transactional. Acquisitions integration takes more time, as you'd have to negotiate new deliverables with all those vendors. And can you really trust all those vendors to work in the best interests of *your* shareholders; for example, would they seek efficiencies that reduce their revenues?

But it's an approach that handles complexity quite well. The brand manager can expand to new countries by buying any needed services there (such as sales, logistics, field service, and government relations). And a new product can utilize all the existing vendors, simply augmenting their scope of work.

I wanted to be able to handle complexity with that same dexterity, but without losing profits and control to other companies' shareholders.

The key is Dean's two Pillars: the business-within-a-business paradigm, and empowerment. This design defines every area of the company as a business operated by an empowered entrepreneur who serves internal (and/or external) customers.

In an organization built on the two Pillars, all our internal functions behave like world-class vendors. They think and act like entrepreneurs, seeking to earn their customers' business by having incredible quality, competitive pricing, and continuous innovation. At least, that's my goal.

That turns out to be the key to addressing every dimension of the cube without having to break up the company into siloed business units.

Everything Is a Shared Service

We dedicate Brand Managers to each of our product lines. But this is not the usual definition of brand management, which is a marketing strategy function. Our Brand Managers have P&L accountabilities for external sales of our products (and marketing is just one of the many services they buy).

Essentially, *everything* else is subcontracted to internal businesses which provide shared services. (In a more bureaucratic culture, you might call them "centers of excellence.") That includes sales, marketing, engineering, manufacturing, logistics, supply chain, customer service, planning and policy, and of course our business office (IT, HR, finance, facilities, procurement, administration, etc.). Each of these functions is a business within the business, selling its products and services internally to the organization (or externally).

This way, we maximize specialization.

All manufacturing sites, for example, report to the global manufacturing leader. If you go to any of our factories, they are identical, with the same processes and standards (except for the differences necessitated by the various product lines). Any improvements in the discipline of manufacturing that are discovered in one plant are immediately replicated to the rest. And I feel more confident knowing our safety and quality protocols are all working the same way in every site. We could not have attained this with a decentralized manufacturing structure reporting to various country or product-line GMs.

Similarly, instead of our Human Resources (HR) function being scattered among business units, we brought all HR professionals together. As a larger group, HR staff can sub-specialize in the various aspects of HR. As a full-service HR consulting business, they provide all the necessary services internally to all customers within our organization. Every other function gets the benefit of their high degree of professional specialization, their internal customer focus, and their entrepreneurial creativity.

The same is true of every function. We currently have 83 internal lines of business (centers of excellence), and no two sell the same service or do the same thing (no overlaps or redundancies). We optimize specialization.

Another big advantage of this integrated approach is that, in all the functions, we have a leader who really understands that profession, and cultivates excellence in each specialty.

Of most importance to me is that our people are really happy. They collaborate daily with people in their same profession (a sub-culture of sorts). People can grow as they are mentored and managed by a boss in their professions. And by consolidating functions into larger, centralized departments, we provide better career paths for all our staff.

Shared *Services* (Not Just Shared Functions)

I've observed that many other companies have some corporate functions at the enterprise level where they consolidate a portion of these shared services. The problem I have seen with most is that these shared "services" act as a control function – as if their job is to oversee and control their internal customers.

Perhaps for this reason, some people I've spoken to (outside our company) are concerned that our structural design – everything a consolidated shared service – will disempower the Brand Managers, with no resources under them and unresponsive corporate services enforcing a "one size fits all" mentality.

But that is far from the case at PDC. Because our structure is based on internal entrepreneurships, everybody knows exactly whom they are serving – their internal customers – for each project or service.

For example, in many companies, CFOs view their jobs as protecting the corporation from irresponsible leaders who want to spend, spend, spend. They take on a controlling role, dictating which costs to cut and which variances to manage. They're happy to take credit for cost savings, but aren't held accountable when other functions fail to deliver what's needed for lack of sufficient resources.

In contrast, we hold *all* our internal entrepreneurs accountable for competitive rates (costs). Our CFO offers financial services to help them achieve this objective – reports, tools, and analyses tailored to their specific needs. While our Financial Services division may offer advice, our empowered business leaders are ultimately accountable for results, and hence have the authority to make the final decisions.

In our company, Brand Managers (and everybody else, too) can get whatever they need from internal entrepreneurs who are eager to serve (not control) them. And all these internal entrepreneurs are willing to tailor their products and services to the unique needs of internal customers (within the bounds of enterprise policies and standards, and with the maximum in reusable intellectual property).

In practice, Brand Managers may have *more* control over the needed functions as customers than they would as bosses over siloed business units. They can buy exactly what they need without having to keep a fixed support group busy, and without the distraction of managing people in so many other professions.

Brand Managers: The Hub of the Wheel

Brand Managers are experts in the markets (the customers) for our products and services. They study what customers need and want, competition, market conditions, and opportunities for product and marketing innovations. They determine strategies for their brands, and are accountable for delivering results (the P&L of their product lines). Figure 3 describes how it works. *(This is not our organization chart.)*

Figure 3: Fully Integrated Organizational Design

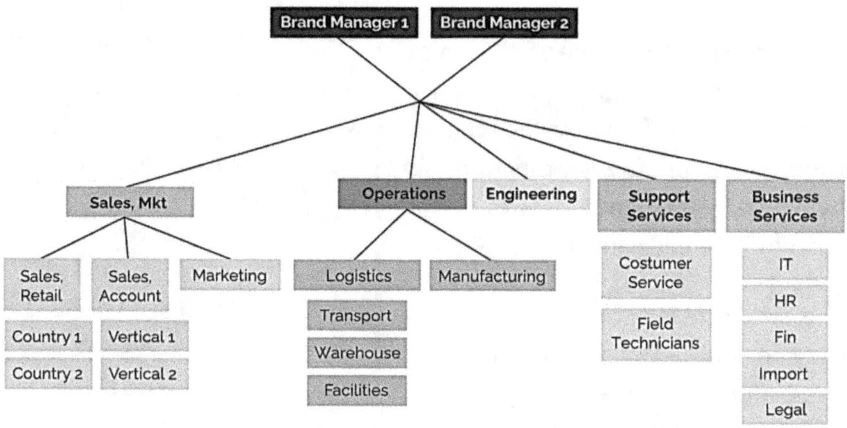

Brand Managers are the "hub of the wheel." But they don't have big organizations.

Brand Managers subcontract for help from anyone, as needed. And those internal subcontractors may, in turn, subcontract to others for help.

All our shared services groups view the Brand Managers as valuable customers whose business they need to earn. All our talent is available wherever they're needed – to any product line, in any country. And solutions are tailored to their needs, and yet with the most possible economies of scale and synergies.

For example, Brand Managers purchase services from Engineering to design their products. They buy manufacturing services from a centralized Manufacturing function, which produces the products they need for their respective markets (e.g., countries). Brand Managers buy warehousing, inventory management, and transportation from a shared Logistics function. Brand Managers purchase sales-as-a-service from a shared Sales organization, and marketing communications such as brand strategy advice and advertising from Marketing. Brand Managers also purchase services from a centralized digital marketing team that serves all brands in all countries. And, of course, Brand Managers buy the range of business services such as IT, Finance, and HR, like everybody else.

Through Brand Managers, the voice of our customers ripples back through our internal value chains. Everybody, in every function, is dynamically aligned with our customers' needs and wants.

> Through Brand Managers, the voice of our customers ripples back through our internal value chains.
>
> Everybody, in every function, is dynamically aligned with our customers' needs and wants.

This structure is entirely scalable. It's easy to add new countries, product lines, and channels – without having to set up new business units, restructure, or make any material change in our operating model.

As we grow, economies of scale improve. Our depth of specialization in each profession increases. Synergies across all the dimensions of the cube are only enhanced. And as a result, performance improves in all countries and all product lines. But the operating model remains stable.

Additionally, our organizational design makes the company very agile. Strategies have to change quickly in our dynamic industry. We're able to reconfigure teams quickly – across brands and countries – to get the best talent across the enterprise serving every brand strategy.

Structure = Organization Chart + Teamwork

An organization made of specialists, of course, requires significant teamwork, which is a critical component of this design. This is why Dean defines the word "structure" as including both the organization chart which determines people's specialties, and the cross-boundary teamwork process that puts these specialists back together to accomplish work.

In conjunction with making everything a shared service, we implemented a dynamic cross-boundary team-formation process called "walk-throughs" (described in Chapter 10).

Our teamwork is boosted by the work we've done on culture (how we behave within this structure), and on our internal economy (our resource-governance processes).

But the key is walk-throughs. They're the glue that joins the company into one organization, and enables the high level of teamwork that makes consolidated shared services work.

Enterprise Synergies

It was amusing.... As we consolidated these shared services, we heard a lot of criticism from the outside world. Pundits constantly warned us that this would not work. But in fact, it did work, beyond anything those "management experts" had seen.

Here's just one example: The old structure had general managers per country. Sales reported to each GM. The problem was that sales processes were different within each country, as each GM saw their business as different and unique.

But actually, at least in our markets, there are more similarities among channels than among countries. In other words, supermarkets are very similar, whether they're in Mexico, Guatemala, or Peru. But their buying patterns are quite different from tienditas (mom-and-pop neighborhood stores) in those same countries.

Within Sales, we established a supermarket leader across the different countries; local supermarket sales leaders report to her. Processes and best practices were standardized. And we immediately saw a substantial jump in sales. The same thing happened with the mom-and-pop channel.

Like the external pundits, our Brand Managers were skeptical at first. They envisioned R&D specific to their category of products reporting to them. They argued that formulating home cleaning chemicals has nothing to do with dairy product R&D.

But in fact, there are a lot of commonalities in the engineering profession, even among the different branches of engineering. All our brands share a common, centralized Engineering service, which designs products ranging from chemicals, to food, to milk products. We now have common development processes that are more reliable, and shared engineering specialties such as packaging and manufacturing engineers. Furthermore, our engineers report to a chief engineer whom they respect, and who knows how to hire, inspire, and manage career engineers.

In the end, centralizing the Engineering function has been key to providing our Brand Managers with a higher quality R&D function, despite the differences in their product lines.

In Manufacturing, we're able to optimize our production capacity at the enterprise level, globally.

We've also seen big benefits in Logistics, where centralized leadership has allowed us to place distribution centers and inventories in the right locations, regardless of country boundaries. This has improved the speed of delivery, and brought down inventory carrying costs. We recurrently compare our "cost-to-serve" by site across the different countries and build strategies to bring all sites to the best benchmarks.

As another form of enterprise synergies, all the talent in the company can be brought to bear on problems anywhere in the company. For example, after we did an acquisition and opened operations in Peru, we ran into a serious problem. Outside observers were quick to suggest that we should appoint a "GM" of Peru to fix it. But that's not our operating model. Instead, all 83 of our talented teams of specialists were engaged, contributing their respective competencies. We had it fixed in just a few months.

Managing Complexity

You might think that having country or product-line GMs is simpler. But down the road, it has significant ongoing costs; it's not scalable; and you'll find yourself forever putting out fires and fixing recurring problems, business unit by business unit.

In fact, our fully integrated organization actually ends up being much simpler. We have one leader for each function globally, responsible for the performance of that internal line of business everywhere. I know exactly who is accountable for every problem and opportunity.

So, how do we manage complexity? How do we ensure focus on, and coordinate across, all those five dimensions of the cube?

Consider the different ways we view and manage our business (Figure 4).

Figure 4: Dimensions of the Cube

➢ Businesses (product and service lines)	Brand Managers
➢ Countries and geographies	Sales, Field Technicians, Government Relations
➢ Sales channels (types of customers)	Sales
➢ Functions (professional specializations)	Everything a shared service
➢ Legal entities	Financial reports, not structure

We have people looking after every dimension of the cube. And we calculate P&L statements for every dimension of the cube.

Of course, our product lines are managed by the Brand Managers.

Countries are still represented. We have Sales presence in every country, of course, all reporting to a global head of Sales.

But our sales force is not strictly geographic. A mom-and-pop store (tiendita) in Guatemala is very similar to one in Peru, but it is quite different from a supermarket. Our Sales department has leaders per sales channel across multiple countries, allowing us to standardize these operations.

Some channels are then divided by country. Relationships with local customers are managed by our geographic sales force. But we also cultivate great relationships with multinational and multi-product customers through our Key Accounts sales representatives whose territories are defined by customers globally.

We also have manufacturing, logistics, field technicians, and other support functions in which localization is important in every country, again all reporting to global leaders. And other functions, like marketing and government relations, may have country specialists in their shared-services groups. So, we can serve each geographic region effectively without any loss of synergies.

Of course, our Brand Managers keep a close eye on results in every country. Despite this real-world complexity, we can view P&Ls by country and by sales channel.

Legal entities are overlaid for tax and regulatory purposes. But they don't affect our day-to-day work. And, of course, we calculate P&Ls for each.

In our weekly and monthly leadership meetings, we review P&Ls from all dimensions – product lines, countries, functions, and legal entities. And where we see problems, we have all the right experts in the room to figure out solutions.

A Caution

This fully integrated organizational structure is incredibly powerful. But again, this organization chart *would not have worked if all we did was a new organization chart*. It is absolutely dependent on fluid, enterprise-wide teamwork.

Remember, this was not simply a restructuring. It was a *transformation*.

In the next four chapters, I'll share our transformation strategy, structural design principles, and the participative change process behind this step in our transformation. I encourage you to pay particular attention to how we implemented high-performance, cross-boundary teamwork (Chapter 10).

7. Transformation Strategy

How did we implement this breakthrough organizational operating model?

Going back in time to the end of the Triage phase, when I realized that real transformation was needed, I also had to become an expert in the "how" – the change processes that implement transformations. I needed the "mechanics."

In studying Dean's work, I came to understand that there's a science of organizational design. There are firm principles, and well-defined constructs (frameworks).

I really liked that rational, engineering approach. And I realized that I had a lot to learn to become an *organizational* leader.

The Organizational "Machine"

As we explored the scope of organizational design, I learned there's a lot more to it than just designing boxes on an organization chart.

> "You do not rise to the level of your goals.
>
> "You fall to the level of your systems."
>
> - James Clear -

I learned to view organizations as systems which send signals that guide people.

I know that some companies grade jobs based (in part) on budget and headcount. Clearly, that's giving people an incentive to maximize their spending and hiring. That job-grading system sends a perverse signal to people, telling them to build empires, not manage costs – the opposite of what we want leaders to do!

The same happens with the traditional approach of setting performance bonuses based on annual profit targets. This encourages managers to negotiate the lowest possible targets, and then over-achieve to secure their bonus. They don't strive for ambitious goals, since that sets them up for potential failure. Sometimes when the Board receives these conservative proposals, it deems them unacceptable, and then sets overly ambitious targets that are equally out of touch with reality. A cycle of fact-free negotiations continues until a compromised middle ground is reached. This is a clear example of how poor systems design sends the wrong signals, and leads to unproductive politics and poor performance.

I saw that if I could get all those signals right, then I could empower people and they'd naturally do the right things, with a minimum of oversight. That alleviated the concern I had about empowerment leading to chaos – at least at the theoretical level.

I asked Dean where these signals come from. He explained the five organizational systems that define an organizational operating model (sometimes called an "organizational ecosystem"), listed in Figure 5. These five systems produce most of the signals that guide staff.

> "...a great manager is essentially an organizational engineer...
>
> "They see their organizations as machines and work assiduously to maintain and improve them."
>
> - Ray Dalio -

Figure 5: Five Organizational Systems [21]

- **Structure**: the organization chart that defines jobs and their specializations, and the cross-boundary teamwork processes that dynamically combine all those functions to get work done.
- **The internal economy**: resource-governance processes, including investment-based budgeting (based on what groups will deliver, not what they'd like to spend), demand management (project intake and priority setting), and accounting.
- **Culture**: Actionable behavioral principles that operationalize values like ethics, integrity, interpersonal relations, productive meetings, cooperation, teamwork, empowerment, customer focus, entrepreneurship, contracts, quality, risk, and feedback.
- **Processes, methods, tools, best practices**: Cross-boundary processes, shared methods and tools, and best practices (like service management and Agile engineering).
- **Metrics and consequences**: Dashboards that help people succeed, and performance metrics that encompass all long- and short-term goals; plus, the consequences of achieving/missing performance metrics, including rewards for exceptional performance and firm, fair performance management.

Organizational Strategy

Our "organizational strategy" includes both a detailed vision of the end-state organization, and a clear path from here to there.

The "clear path" was the sequence of changes we planned to make in those five organizational systems to transform our organization.

I was excited by the potential, and eager to make all the changes. But Dean cautioned me not to try to work on more than one organizational system at a time. Each would engage the leadership team in learning and a participative design process. Meanwhile, they had a business to run; so, they only had a limited amount of time to spend on transformation.

As eager as I was to get it all right, I agreed to prioritize the organizational systems, and do each with excellence.

So, the question was, where do we start?

Step 1: Structure

I thought about my many concerns, and began to see which organizational systems were most likely to be their root causes. Organizational structure kept coming up again and again.

In most companies I've observed, the structure evolves over time without conscious design. As the company grows, new departments and groups pop up like weeds.

To make matters worse, most leaders don't like to address people's performance issues (especially firing people for poor performance). Instead of confronting the problem head on, they change the organization's structure, and divide responsibilities so that a more capable person can assume what the poor performer couldn't do.

Changes are made to solve a specific problem, or to resolve an individual issue. There is no process, no principles, no logic. With nobody taking care of the garden, you end up with weeds all over the place. If you let this go on for years, you end up with a jungle.

Structure for us was just that – a jungle. We were in desperate need of a landscape architect! We came from a siloed, decentralized organization. The business-unit leaders had each designed their own jungle below them, without any consistency, any design principles, or even any common design language.

There were no clear centers of excellence. Professions were decentralized into small groups of generalists who couldn't possibly perform as well as centralized specialists would. A function in one business unit didn't necessarily deliver the same services as a function of the same name in another business unit.

Accountabilities were unclear, which undermined both employee engagement and results. And with vague and broad responsibilities, people were trying to do too many things and couldn't possibly do any of them with excellence.

And cross-departmental teamwork was poor.

I also saw that we were completely lacking in some critical competencies, such as customer service, organizational design, strategic planning, and compensation design, to name a few. When we inventoried all the necessary competencies, it turns out people thought somebody else was doing them; but in the end, no one was.

We needed to design an organization that would include all the competencies we needed, then and as far into the future as we could see (someone responsible for functions, however small today, to be accountable for our occasional needs in the short term and to drive growth). And, of course, we needed clear accountabilities to know who would own each competency – each business within a business.

Beyond Structure

Clearly, we needed to restructure our organization. But in truth, we needed much more than a new organization chart. Remember, we needed a *transformation* – a new organizational operating model, an entirely different way of doing business.

Culture

I knew we also had a lot of work to do on culture. But I understood from the framework that fixing the structure would, in part, introduce important behavioral changes, building a culture of entrepreneurship and empowerment. Then, we could do a more comprehensive job of culture later.

Internal Economy

And I knew we'd have to rethink our resource-governance processes – what Dean calls the "internal economy" – to reinforce a business-within–business structure. This, too, is critical to ownership thinking, and to teamwork.

Teamwork breaks down when an internal supplier is restricted by their budget, but their customers keep demanding more services. Those customers will find some other way to get the job done.

Teamwork is also impeded if one group's highest priority is another group's lowest. That occurs when each manager sets priorities for their own resources. Priorities must be aligned across the enterprise.

In a market-based internal economy, the supplier is responsible for offering competitive rates (unit costs). But customers are responsible for volume; they decide what they "purchase." So, ultimately, it's up to customers to pay for what they get (whether the money is channeled to the supplier via its budget or on a fee-for-service basis).

For example, let's say HR's recruiting service has a unit rate of $100 per person hired. The company initially estimated hiring 50 people in one recent quarter, which would amount to a $5,000 budget for recruiting in HR. However, by mid quarter, things have changed and our internal customers now need to hire 150 people because of a new site that was acquired. We can't expect the HR department to recruit 150 people with the original $5,000 budget. The customer (who will benefit from the work of HR) decides the volume (150 people). With that authority comes accountability. The customer must provide a budget of $15,000 (150 x $100) to HR. Then, HR can get the resources it needs (perhaps through contractors); and there's no need for that customer to look elsewhere for recruiting services, or to try to do it themselves.

And when customers fund their purchases, they fund the entire project team. Thus, everybody needed on the team has the time and resources to contribute. Priorities are aligned.

(Funding is provided through our quarterly budgeting process, not cross-charges.)

These changes to our internal economy were necessary to make enterprisewide teamwork work.

Metrics

Treating our managers as internal entrepreneurs has a big impact on performance metrics, too. Note, for example, that typical metrics make managers responsible for budget variances. This is counter to internal entrepreneurship and teamwork. It forces managers to turn away additional business (which would force them to spend more and hence cause a "negative" variance) since they're expected to "come in on budget."

Instead, we manage people based on (break-even) P&Ls. When customers buy more, suppliers' costs go up; but so do their revenues.

Furthermore, it's certainly not enough to measure people just on P&Ls and project/service delivery (such as OKRs) or on how they deliver their products and services (KPIs).

Instead, managers should be measured on *all* the things an entrepreneur must succeed at to earn customers' business. Figure 6 offers examples of entrepreneurial metrics.

We needed a comprehensive view of performance metrics to reinforce internal entrepreneurship.

Figure 6: Entrepreneurial Metrics [22]

- Customer satisfaction
- Market share
- Your group's break-even P&L targets (but not budget variances)
- Competitive rates (unit costs)
- Profit targets on external sales (selected groups)
- Product/service quality
- Reliability, integrity
- Safety and compliance
- Innovation
- Viability of your group's business strategies
- Compliance with, and contribution to, our organizational operating model
- Employee engagement and satisfaction
- Supplier relationships (especially internal suppliers)
- Positive contribution to the community

Structure First

I knew our transformation into the business-within-a-business paradigm would take more than a restructuring. But our structure was at the point of crisis. It was causing confusion, unclear accountabilities, impossible jobs, stress among departments, and poor cross-boundary teamwork. We needed a restructuring to fix the root causes of those problems.

This led me to decide that the first step in our transformation strategy had to be organizational structure. So, we deferred any further work on culture, our internal economy, and metrics.

8. Principle-based Approach to Structure

As I said, I'm a life-long learner. When it came to embarking on an organizational restructuring, my first step was to study the literature on organizational design. As I mentioned earlier, I read many books on the topic. It was frustrating:

- Many rehashed the old "Star" model where structure and strategy are intertwined. I knew that we needed to be far more agile, and certainly could not afford to restructure any time that any of our multifaceted strategies change. (More on this below.)
- Some described a matrix, where people have two bosses: one to manage their profession, and the other to manage their work. But we need to deploy our talent more flexibly; our talent serves multiple projects at once. And we certainly can't afford to restructure every time our strategic initiatives list changes. (I discussed other problems with matrix organizations in Chapter 5.)
- I read about Holacracy, which seemed to me to be a "take your hands off the wheel" approach where people have no bosses, and can specialize in whatever they want and offer their services wherever they want. As far as I can tell, they have no guarantee of having all the needed specialties represented somewhere in the company. Performance management is very difficult. And many bureaucratic processes are required to support teamwork and keep the chaos within reasonable limits.
- There are a few cases of companies that went to the extreme and made every group a profit center (e.g., Haier, Disco). Internal customers pay market prices, and are allowed to work around internal support services and hire vendors and consultants directly. Internal functions could go out of business, leaving the enterprise at the mercy of vendors. And again, can they be sure they have available all the needed competencies, now and into the future?
- I saw some people proposing that structure should be based on process engineering (the "socio-technical systems" approach, or

"service management"). But, of course, there's a lot more to our work than routine, well-structured processes. And processes crisscross the organization; many processes require the same kinds of talent, and we can't afford to replicate a group of specialists for each distinct process.

- The case studies I read describe various alternative designs, perhaps with pros and cons. But they lack principles, and ultimately provide little in the way of clear guidance.

Perhaps this is why most CEOs tend to make decisions by intuition. They present a high-level organization chart to the Board. The Board reviews it in a brief discussion. And the decision is made.

But what is the logic behind those designs?

Structure Not Based on People

To me, it was very clear that it would not be wise to design a structure around the people we had at the time (as so many leaders do). For most leaders, it's uncomfortable to make tough people-decisions. So, many adjust the structure to accommodate the limitations of the incumbent leaders.

But then, when a leader changes jobs, it's very hard to find a replacement who exactly matches the talents of the former incumbent. So, the next leader in that job (which was tailored to their predecessor) is likely to perform poorly. It's either that, or you restructure with every leadership change.

Furthermore, synergies are lost when staff are assembled into groups based on the interests of a leader rather than their professional commonalities.

Structure Not Based on Strategy

It became equally clear that we didn't want to design our organization around our business *strategy* (as in that 1960s axiom, "structure follows strategy"). [23]

In fact, we pursue multiple strategies at any point in time. It doesn't make sense to pick one as the basis for structure, and then try to fit the rest in.

Even more salient, today's business climate is not stable and predictable, as perhaps it was in the 1960s. We live in a world that's volatile, uncertain, complex, and ambiguous (VUCA). Agility is critical. We must be able to rally our capabilities around new strategies quickly.

As Dean says, "An organization designed around today's business strategies will not only fail at tomorrow's strategies; it will fail to *discover* tomorrow's strategies."

If we designed our structure based on business strategies, we'd find ourselves continually restructuring, which would be costly, chaotic, and unproductive.

My goal was an agile organization that could not only succeed at executing multiple parallel strategies, but also reconfigure itself quickly to address ever-changing strategies. Beyond that, I wanted an organization that could generate new business strategies dynamically in response to changing business conditions and opportunities.

> "Instead of trying to predict Black Swan events, focus on building systems that can thrive in the face of such unpredictability."
>
> - Nassim Nicholas Taleb -

My experience tells me that it is much more important to prioritize organizational strategy over business strategy. Organizational strategy will provide the "machine" that can respond to ever-changing market conditions and new opportunities, and can generate ever-changing business strategies. The key is to design a structure that can do this continually over time, not a structure tuned to today's business strategies.

Principle-based Design

I firmly believe in an organizational design based on principles (not personalities, opinions, imitating other companies, or near-term strategies and imperatives). This is the only path to a lasting, robust design – a design that will evolve consistently over time without the need for repeated restructurings.

I understood that organizations are complex, integrated systems, where every part of the design is interconnected. Dabbling with structure without principles, and without an understanding of systemic problems that result from those structure decisions, is dangerous. For example, it's easy to combine functions in a way that creates conflicts of interests, or biases a function to favor some of its customers over others. The challenge of structure is whole-system design.

Principles also provide a basis for engaging the leadership team in the design process, without discussions descending into political battles. We argue design questions based on the principles, not what individual leaders want in their groups.

> "When making rules, explain the principles behind them."
>
> - Ray Dalio -

However, I am certainly not an organizational engineer.

What I found in Dean's work was a principle-based approach, along with a well-tested change management process, that addressed all the requirements of our multi-business, multi-country company. I felt confident this was the path to a logical, scalable structure.

Principles of Structure

I had already come to believe in the business-within-a-business paradigm. So, I knew that the boxes on our organization chart had to be defined as internal lines of business.

And, of course, I was committed to empowerment.

Those two Pillars were the first and last of the seven principles of structure that Dean's studies revealed (Figure 7).

Figure 7: Seven Principles of Structure [24]

- **Principle 1: Empowerment (the Golden Rule)**: Authorities and accountabilities must match.
- **Principle 2: Specialization and Teamwork**: Maximize performance by optimizing specialization; but you can't specialize if you can't team.
- **Principle 3: Precise Domains**: Define clear boundaries, with no overlaps or gaps.
- **Principle 4: Basis for Substructure**: Divide a function into sub-groups based on what it's supposed to be good at (sub-specialties within each specialty).
- **Principle 5: Avoid Conflicts of Interests**: Don't expect people to go in two opposing directions.
- **Principle 6: Cluster by Professional Synergies**: Cluster groups under a common boss based on similar professions.
- **Principle 7: Business Within a Business**: Every group is defined as a business whose job is to satisfy customers (internal and external) with products and services.

All seven Principles guided our restructuring.

9. Our Restructuring Process

Most CEOs want consultants to implement quick-fixes. But as I've said, I was looking for more than just a new organization chart. I was after a fundamental change in the company's operating model – its structure, work-flows, culture, and metrics – and in the way our staff thought about their jobs.

I understood that a real transformation in an organization, and in people's thinking and behaviors, is a complex multi-year transformation process. I understood that to be a transformational leader, I'd need to be patient; and I'd need to invest.

I also realized that we needed to think "outside the box." Simply moving some boxes around would not have changed much. I wanted to build the structure around internal lines of business, not our existing poorly defined functions and roles. To achieve that, I decided to start the design of our organization chart with a *clean sheet of paper*, to maximize our creative thinking.

> "...redesigning the system [starts by] asking yourself, what would you do right now if you could do whatever you wanted to. Because if you don't know what you would do if you could do whatever you wanted to, how in the world can you know what you would do under constraints!?"
>
> - Dr. Russell Ackoff [25] -

To that end, Dean helped me lay out our restructuring project plan – and it was unlike anything I'd ever seen.

Participative

Our structure was not designed by me alone. I engaged my entire leadership team in the process.

Sure, this was expensive (in terms of their time). But it was absolutely necessary.

To achieve a real transformation – into an empowered, entrepreneurial organization – all our leaders, at every level, had to learn to think and act like entrepreneurs.

That requires a real commitment from our leaders to change. And it requires that they understand our new organizational operating model well enough to teach and implement it.

To get our leaders onboard and understanding a radically different operating model well enough to teach it, and to get them thinking and behaving very differently, we had to engage them in a participative restructuring process.

Organizational Engineering Function

I knew I would not have the time to personally plan and facilitate every aspect of the change process. So, one of the first things I did was appoint a leader of Organizational Engineering (OE, sometimes called Organizational Excellence or Organizational Effectiveness) – essentially a transformation guru and project manager.

This is not a temporary position, just for the duration of the restructuring process. Like a garden, you need to continually fertilize and weed it. I have found that few companies invest in people dedicated to organizational excellence. This is like having a beautiful garden designed by a great landscape architect, and then never tending to it. Years later, you'll again have a jungle.

We invested in a dedicated team of organizational engineers (OE) who are constantly refining the structure and our processes as we grow. They help us continually further the transformation, and adapt as things change. We couldn't keep up with our pace of growth and repeatedly integrate acquisitions if it weren't for this OE line of business.

The "Rainbow Analysis"

At the beginning of the process, I told all leaders that they would lose their titles. (We were designing the new structure starting with a blank sheet of paper, so there were no titles yet.) You could hear a pin drop when I delivered that message! Everyone was in shock. But I promised them that nobody would lose their employment because of restructuring. This gave us the flexibility to design the best structure possible.

Figure 8: Types of Internal Businesses: The Building Blocks of Structure [26]

- **Service Providers**: sell ongoing services
  - **Asset-based**: ongoing services produced by assets, including operations; and brand-management of off-the-shelf products
  - **People-based**: ongoing services produced primarily by people, such as customer service and the various support services

- **Engineers**: sell new solutions
  - **Applications**: purpose-specific solutions (our products)
  - **Base**: purpose-independent solutions, i.e., the components that go into applications (e.g., manufacturing engineering, packaging engineering)

- **Coordinators**: facilitate consensus on shared decisions (e.g., plans and policies, organizational engineering, product standards, regulatory compliance, business continuity, security)

- **Sales and Marketing**: link the organization to customers

- **Audit**: inspect, judge, and perhaps veto others

Our first step was to analyze our current organization chart and list the lines of business under each manager.

To do that, Dean trained us in a framework of all the types of businesses that exist inside any organization (Figure 8). Note that they're all defined by what they sell, not what they do.

We translated this generic framework into our industry. Then, each of our leaders listed the lines of business under them. This was the first step in their learning to understand their jobs as entrepreneurs.

We color-coded the different types of internal businesses. And I'll tell you, it was quite a colorful chart! (That's why Dean calls this the "Rainbow Analysis.") You'll see it in Figure 9. Don't worry about reading it; I include it only to show you the multiple colors under each leader, and the way colors were scattered around the organization chart.

Figure 9: Our Rainbow Organization Chart

That graphically illustrated our structural problems: groups going too many directions at once (sometimes with conflicting objectives); and lines of business scattered across the enterprise (missing synergies).

We also realized there were many missing lines of business.

This Rainbow Analysis confirmed in all our minds the need for change – well, with all honesty, in *most* of our leaders' minds.

Lines of Business

The Rainbow Analysis gave us a list of the lines of business that existed within the organization at that time. But what about the lines of business we were missing? It was an eye opener for all of us to discover that everybody thought someone else was responsible for a certain activity, and after surveying the room, we found that actually there was nobody providing those functions.

The framework of types of businesses (the Building Blocks) helped us brainstorm additional lines of business that we needed right away, or knew we'd need in the future. It didn't matter whether they warranted full-time staff, or were to be fulfilled with contractors and vendors. Someone had to lead each of those businesses, even if they were part-time jobs (such as managing a vendor's services). Every capability that the enterprise was going to need had to be assigned somewhere.

In a very interactive workshop with the leadership team, we listed them.

This gave us a comprehensive list of all the lines of business that had to be designed into the new organization chart, sorted by Building Block.

Clustering the Lines of Business

The next step was to cluster those lines of business into tier-one boxes (reporting to me, the CEO).

We talked about the principle, "You can't specialize if you can't team." As I had already done, the leadership team committed to investing in great cross-boundary teamwork. We promised ourselves that we'd learn how to get everybody working with everybody through teamwork, not the organization chart. That way, we didn't have to put people under a common boss just because they frequently work together (creating silos).

This allowed us to cluster all similar lines of business together (a.k.a., "centers of excellence") under a common boss who knows their profession, manages their performance, and coaches and inspires them.

In those days, we were working with sticky-notes on flip charts. We moved the sticky-notes (representing lines of business) around to create clusters that we believed would optimize synergies.

This workshop benefited from firm facilitation. We debated each move based on the seven Principles, not based on the way we did it in the past, the way other companies are organized, or individual leaders' interests and intuitions. And we made every decision by consensus.

When we were done considering everybody's ideas for moving sticky-notes around, the resulting clusters of lines of business represented tier-one jobs.

This participative process was designed to ensure that we had the commitment of our entire leadership team to a radically different organizational structure.

Selecting Leaders

At this point in the process, we had designed the tier-one boxes (reporting to me) on the future organization chart. I then interviewed and selected leaders for each of the boxes.

Even this step was participative. I met with each member of the leadership team (including people at lower tiers of the hierarchy who were interested in senior leadership jobs). We discussed their career aspirations and where they'd like to be in the new organization chart. Their input guided me in the selection of my new tier-one leaders.

Domains

As Principle 3 suggests, a few words in a box don't really tell you what business a group is in, or where the boundaries between groups are.

So, our next step was to craft "domains." Domains define (in a paragraph or two) exactly what lines of business are in each group.

This established clear, precise boundaries. We ensured there were no gaps (missing lines of business) or overlaps (internal redundancies and competition).

We all followed a set of clear guidelines on how to craft our domains. There was no vague and bureaucratic language like "roles and responsibilities." It was all about defining what each group *sells*.

This step alone drove a huge paradigm shift. Writing their domains got leaders to look at their jobs in a different way – not as managing the resources under them, but rather as running a business that serves customers (internal and external) by producing results (products and services).

Tiers

We defined the organization chart in two steps:

First, we designed and formed the tier-one leadership team, reporting to me. The selected tier-one leaders crafted their domains.

With a clearer understanding of their future jobs, the tier-one leaders then designed the tier-two structure (reporting to them) by dividing the lines of business under them into sub-clusters, which became boxes on the organization chart at the next level.

Tier-one leaders participated in the selection of tier-two leaders. They did this as a team, so that we could put the best qualified leaders from anywhere in the company in each box. I feared this would be contentious. In fact, it was not. The clear domains and knowledge of people's talents overruled any attempts by leaders to claim the "best" people.

We had to leave some of the boxes open for lack of the right talent. These became targets for external recruiting or internal career development.

Of course, we engaged tier-two leaders in crafting their domains, developing their understanding of their new jobs as internal entrepreneurships.

Catalogs

To further understand each domain (box on the organization chart) as a business within a business, the next step was to develop catalogs of each leader's specific products and services.

This was challenging as well. People wanted to talk about what they *do* (not sell), or their competencies – as in conventional job descriptions.

To really describe our products and services, leaders had to think strictly about *what their (internal) customers would own or consume* as a result of their work – things that customers can choose to buy from them.

This not only enhanced their ownership thinking. It brought about a focus on results (rather than processes), and an appreciation of the value delivered by each group.

Walk-throughs

When we designed the new organization chart, we knew it wouldn't work without great teamwork. We understood that the higher the degree of specialization (which results from the consolidation of shared services), the greater the need for excellence in cross-boundary teamwork.

The leadership team did not want to simply announce the organization chart, and then struggle (in public view) to figure out how to get it to work. Another fear was that if we didn't all understand and agree on who is accountable for what within a project team, the organization would revert back into self-sufficient silos, despite what the organization chart said.

Our goal was to understand how real work will get done in the new organization *before* go-live.

Therefore, the next step was to practice "walk-throughs" – our cross-boundary team-formation process. So, before we implemented the new structure, the leadership team spent many hours together practicing walk-throughs.

Walk-throughs are so important that they deserve their own chapter (coming up next).

This turned out to be the most challenging (and time consuming) step in the restructuring process. But it was absolutely necessary. By the time we deployed the new structure, everyone on the leadership team had a reasonably good idea of how it would actually work in real life. In retrospect, I wish we had done even more practice walk-throughs back then. But we did "hit the ground running."

Final Steps

Once the leadership team fully understood how the new structure would work (after all those walk-throughs), we were on the home stretch.

We assigned all our staff (including contractors), assets, and vendor contracts to the appropriate groups. And we planned the enterprisewide go-live very carefully.

After go-live, we asked everybody to keep doing everything they had been doing (even if it didn't fit their new domains) until accountabilities were properly "migrated." We used an explicit process to migrate accountabilities from people to the appropriate groups if those projects or services no longer fit their new domains, with one-on-one discussions of what the receiving group needs from the person who had been doing the work in order to accept accountability (documentation, training, etc.). This ensured that no commitments were missed in the transition.

Timeframe

In its entirety, the restructuring process took close to two years. But that's okay.

There's a saying, "Measure twice, cut once." Well, I'd say that given the level of effort we've put into the transformation so far (and our investment is continuing), we measured *ten* times before cutting! That's because the costs of getting it wrong are high – not just the downside of the repeated restructurings (the pendulum swings that damage the culture, productivity, and morale), but the very effectiveness of the enterprise.

I'm confident that given the investment we've made in a participative, principle-based design, we will never again need to pay the costs of a comprehensive restructuring.

10. Cross-boundary Teamwork

As I've said, I wanted to maximize enterprise performance, and that meant maximizing specialization.

Of course, specialization requires teamwork. If their cross-boundary teamwork processes are weak, they're forced to create "silo" organizations with professions scattered among the self-sufficient business units (leading to less specialization).

Or they install a "generalists" function (e.g., in IT, an "enterprise architect") who is accountable for putting all the pieces together, but may or may not be an expert in, and hence not suitable to be accountable for, an end result; these generalists disempower other groups whose products they take over.

Our goal of maximizing specialization necessitated investing in great cross-boundary teamwork. In short, to be a fully integrated organization where everything is a shared service, we'd have to get really good at forming teams across the entire enterprise, and those teams had to be high-performing.

High-performance Teamwork

"High-performance teamwork" means assembling just the right people, at just the right time, with clear individual accountabilities, and a clear chain of command. (See Figure 10.)

Teams should form dynamically, based on the needs of each project. And they should come together without the need for management intervention – without expecting the executive who controls all the needed specialists to form teams.

Figure 10: Definition of High-performance Teamwork [27]

- **Just the right people**: Teams should form dynamically based on the unique needs of each distinct project or service (not a fixed, engineered process or the same team for every project). Every team needs to include all the needed specialists, regardless of where in the organization they may report.

- **Just the right time**: Team members don't need to be there for the entire project. Once they have delivered their value (e.g., advice, subcomponents, support services), they can leave the team and move on to other priorities.

- **Clear individual accountabilities**: "All for one, and one for all" doesn't respect the unique competencies of the various specialists on a team. And shared accountabilities often lead to confusion about who's in charge and finger-pointing. While team spirit (and helping one another) is valuable, clear individual accountabilities for deliverables (products or services) within a team is essential.

- **Clear chain of command**: One group must be accountable for the entire project or service, and manage and assemble the deliverables from the rest of the team members.

Self-forming teams are very important to me. On complex projects that need diverse specialists, that executive where all the needed functions meet may be me, the CEO. If I had to be the one putting teams together, I'd certainly become a bottleneck, slowing the entire organization down.

> "A stable organization, combined with an agile process for assembling just the right capabilities for each initiative, is the best way to handle a VUCA world."
>
> - N. Dean Meyer -

Meanwhile, it would drag me down to a tactical level, rather than focusing on strategies where I'm most needed and add the most value.

This would be contrary to what I am trying to achieve – a company that can work better every day without me.

How Teams Form in a Business-within-a-business Organization

The business-within-a-business paradigm we'd adopted gave us the process of team-formation we were looking for. Dean taught us a method he calls "walk-throughs." Walk-throughs give us the ability to quickly assemble all the right specialties to address new challenges, now and in the future. This is the essence of *agility*.

Our walk-throughs are much like the playbook of a professional sports team. Great players alone don't guarantee victory; success comes from practicing and mastering how to move as one, with precision and clarity. Each walk-through was an entry in our play-book, and our way of rehearsing those plays. Walk-throughs ensure that every specialist knows their role, their timing, and how their part contributes to the team's overall win.

This method is not only critical to getting shared services to work. It was an essential part of the transformation of people's thinking.

Essentially, walk-throughs map out our internal value chains dynamically for each unique project and service.

Figure 11 explains how it works.

During the restructuring process, the leadership team practiced many hypothetical walk-throughs – projects underway, others that they anticipated, and ongoing services. Then, after go-live, we use walk-throughs to put together all new project teams.

Figure 11: Steps in a Walk-through [28]

1. Identify exactly what deliverable the (internal or external) customer wishes to buy.

2. Identify which domain (leader) "sells" that product/service. This is the "prime contractor."

3. Ask the prime contractor what help (products and services) they need from other groups. These are "subcontractors" (internal groups, not vendors).

4. Subcontractors, in turn, get a chance to request help from other groups – subs to subcontractors.

Example of a Walk-through

For example, when we introduce a new product, we have one person responsible for the P&L of that product line; that individual is the "prime contractor" responsible for the new product launch. In our organizational structure, this is the Brand Manager described in Chapter 6.

They first need to assess the market, so they buy market research from our Marketing group. They may also buy competitive research to see what else is out there. This helps them define the product and the pricing.

Remember: When I say "buy," I do not mean that we charge one another. This is just our way of clarifying internal customer-supplier relationships.

Of course, to get the funding to invest in a new product, they need to explain the costs. They buy a study from our Engineers (product designers) which suggests alternatives, and for each option, development costs, ongoing costs, pros and cons, risks, etc.

When the time comes, those product engineers may need help from other supporting Engineering disciplines to actually develop the product. For example, they likely will need help with packaging. So, at this proposal stage, they need to subcontract with other Engineers for their sub-proposals (costs, etc.).

Especially with our food products, they may need help from our Regulatory Compliance group to analyze regulatory requirements.

And to estimate ongoing (life-cycle) costs, they'll need to subcontract for input from Manufacturing and Logistics.

Manufacturing may, in turn, subcontract to Manufacturing Engineering to get an estimate of the plant and equipment required to produce the product. They'll have to amortize any needed capital into their life-cycle cost estimates.

Manufacturing may need help from our Procurement group to get estimates of raw materials costs.

Of course, Brand Managers will need to subcontract to Sales, Marketing, Customer Service, and others for their cost estimates, to include their ongoing costs in this analysis.

With that information, Brand Managers assemble a proposal – a business plan. I then have all the information I need to decide whether to fund the initiative, in the context of our strategies, our financials, and other investments we're making.

If I do fund it, Brand Managers buy product development from the Engineer (the same one who developed the proposal). That Engineer assembles the same team of subcontractors – this time to actually design the product.

Once designed, the Brand Manager buys operational services like marketing, sales, manufacturing, warehousing, delivery, customer service, inventory management, and so on.

The modularity of the design makes it agile and scalable. You see how we can marshal all the right competencies to get the best possible results on every initiative.

The Results of Walk-throughs

These days, the right people come together on teams without my having to intervene.

I appreciate the clear accountabilities. I know who's accountable for the entire initiative. And within teams, everybody involved knows their specific accountabilities for sub-deliverables (components of the solution or support services).

If there are any disputes within the team, the prime contractor (in the above example, the Brand Manager) has the final say (and the ultimate accountability). So, teams are self-managing; they rarely need to appeal to a higher authority to make decisions or resolve differences.

Admittedly, we have more work to do. We need to further practice and refine our walk-throughs. But generally we are getting the right specialists involved in every project and service, and people know what they're accountable for, and to whom. Agile, high-performance teamwork is happening.

We have empowered our leaders, clarified accountabilities for results, built the teamwork process, and now the organization has taken on a life of its own without my having to get involved in tactical issues.

In fact, I'm constantly amazed at how much gets done without my involvement. The more the organization matures, the less I speak.

> I'm constantly amazed at how much gets done without my involvement.
>
> The more the organization matures, the less I speak.

11. Business Results So Far

What we did with our organizational design was certainly not typical; and what we achieved was far from typical. Many questioned our bold, and at times risky, approach. But the results tell a compelling story.

When I took on the CEO job in 2011, I thought we had profits of $834K. However, I quickly learned that the books were cooked, and we had a lot of problems swept under the rug in the balance sheet.

After I cleaned up the balance sheet, we posted a $2.2M net loss in 2012.

This negative result obviously caught the bank's attention, and I was immediately called in to explain. I told the bank executive that we were in the middle of a transformation process, and that things would get worse before they got better.

> "...company CEOs and boards of directors should resist the undue pressure of quarterly earnings, and it is clearly somewhat their fault when they don't.
>
> "[They] take short-term actions to increase earnings, such as ... cutting certain investments that may be terrific but can show accounting losses in the first year or two.... This could put you on a treadmill to ruin."
>
> - Jamie Dimon [29] -
> Chairman and CEO, JPMorgan Chase

My prediction was correct. In 2013, we posted a $4.2M net loss. This was partly the result of our further cleaning of the balance sheet, and partly due to the time and money we were investing in the transformation.

Facing poor results, not every CEO would invest in transformation. But I knew that it would be the key to our future profitability and growth. I did not succumb to the pressures of quarterly results. (It didn't hurt that we are a privately-held company, and my Board is very supportive.)

Sales have grown from $89M to $430M in the 15 years since we started the transformation. However, I constantly remind our team that sales is not our most important metric. (We use Economic Value Added as the only indicator of value creation.) We have actually let go over $100M in sales of non-strategic contracts during these 15 years. To forgo revenues is counterintuitive at first, as we lose scale. But not all sales are strategic and add value. Profitability, however, has continued to climb as we remain focused on value creation.

We have grown our EBITDA (earnings before interest, taxes, depreciation, and amortizations) at a rate of 33% per year (Figure 12), which translates to a doubling of value every 2.2 years, or 29x since the beginning of the transformation.

This, of course, represents significant wealth creation not only for our original shareholders, but also for all our leaders who have participated in our Employee Equity Program.

Figure 12: Our Sales Growth

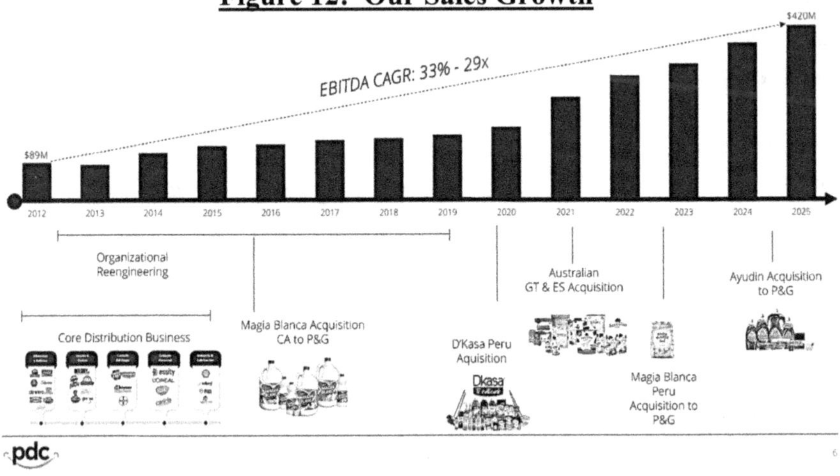

While we're on the topic of financial results, I note that we've achieved empowerment (key to our growth) without any loss of financial control. Our organizational operating model has developed business acumen at all levels. It's enhanced (not eroded) our financial controls.

All 160 leaders meet 20 minutes weekly to forecast how we will close the month, the quarter, and the year. Leaders within each domain are able to do this with precision. Today, by week 3 of each month, we already have an estimate of how each line of the P&L will close, and with 96% accuracy, the net profit for the month. This gives us a chance to implement gap-closing actions before the month ends.

We also have excellent controls at the strategic level. Because our growth rate is so fast and the dynamics of our business are changing at a rapid pace, our original annual strategic planning method was too slow. Our priorities end up changing significantly by mid-year. We had to develop planning methods that could keep up with an ever-changing strategic landscape.

Today, as a key element of our dynamic planning processes, on a quarterly basis, we construct a rolling 3-year plan with a detailed plan for the next quarter.

Despite our dynamic approach to business strategy, our organizational structure and operating model have stayed relatively stable. It's an agile, scalable structure – by design.

We've rebuilt ourselves from the ground up, evolving from a bankrupt company into a thriving, profitable organization, driven by our core purpose: *to transform lives*. We are achieving extraordinary results in a mature industry, which is always tough. Our differentiator is operational excellence, which we have been able to achieve through an innovative organizational design.

In the next six chapters, I'll describe in more detail the benefits of our transformation – the factors which generated these business results.

12. Example of Benefits: Talent

To me, a very important benefit of our organizational design is its impact on our people. So, I'll discuss this first in a series of six chapters that describe the many benefits of our transformation.

Some People Fell by the Wayside

I'm sad to say that the impact on people was not always positive. Even after the initial purge of ethics and performance problems, not all the remaining leaders survived. Many of our original leaders couldn't, or wouldn't, get onboard, despite having been in the room when we designed the structure.

Even those who were willing to support the transformation weren't always qualified to lead in this new paradigm. I've learned to look for different traits in leaders....

What we really need are people who are humble, grounded, life-long learners, compassionate, and humanistic. I have no interest in working with arrogant people; I believe such people are less capable of learning, and do not make good coaches of empowered subordinates.

I look for strategic thinkers who can see where we need to go and what we need to do to get there.

I look for systems thinkers who can trace problems to root causes, and fix the organizational impediments to success.

We need people who understand (or can quickly learn) the language of finance.

And particularly challenging to find, we need people with an entrepreneurial spirit, who understand that they're running internal businesses that serve internal and external customers, and accept accountability for delivering results (not just managing resources and processes). To me, entrepreneurial thinking is more important than functional skills, which can be learned.

> "Push them to greatness or push them out the door."
>
> - Ron Lovett -

Many of our original leaders just weren't able to think like entrepreneurs, or they wouldn't accept accountability for results. I did my best to bring them along. But in the end, some left voluntarily; some I had to let go.

In total, almost 50% of the leaders left within the first year, and over 80% of the original leadership team were gone by the three-year milestone. I'm told that this is extraordinarily high. Perhaps this was because the company had been so badly managed (by a series of CEOs) in the past. Too many leaders enjoyed authority (power) without accountabilities, and didn't want to give that up. Some had been promoted beyond their level of competence. And a few didn't live up to our high ethical standards.

I felt terrible for all the people who lost their jobs. However, I knew it was the right thing to do for the company and the remaining employees.

Even more difficult was recruiting talent into all these new leadership positions. We designed an equity program which helped attract top talent and reinforce our ownership culture. And our new organizational operating model, with its empowerment, teamwork, and entrepreneurship, also helped attract top candidates.

I made many mistakes. Some of my selections were poor. And perhaps more significantly, our onboarding of new leaders was not always successful.

For example, I hired a CFO who came from a large telecommunications company, and a Vice President of Sales from an international beverage company. They came from traditional, bureaucratic organizations, and couldn't get their minds around internal entrepreneurship.

They also lacked a skill I consider essential to leadership. Executives from companies that were already working and profitable had never had the experience of designing an organization, its processes, and its culture. They would complain that “nothing works here."

I would reply, “Exactly! That’s why I hired you.”

They never really understood that organizational design is a fundamental responsibility (and competency) of leadership. They may have been technically competent, but we need systems thinking, teamwork, and entrepreneurship just as much as functional excellence. They too had to go.

The biggest problem with most external hires was that they didn’t share our culture. We really tried to bring them onboard; but most had learned how to maneuver corporate organizations from their years of experience in bureaucratic, political, and toxic cultures. They were extremely capable professionals, but exhibited terrible behaviors (like micro-managing activities rather than results, or refusing to take accountability for results). We couldn't allow this.

Growing Our Own Leaders: The Scholars Program

As a result of the challenges associated with changing deeply ingrained behaviors in senior leaders coming in from outside, we are now focused on developing leaders internally (whenever possible).

We have a program called “Scholars,” to which 500 recent graduates (mostly Engineers) apply annually. Applicants go through an intense two-day interview process. We select between five and seven of the applicants (1.5% acceptance rate). Then, they go through a multi-year training process where they are given important responsibilities and projects within different areas.

Oscar Mejia, who leads Business Services including HR, created and implemented this program. He himself came from a similar program in his first job at P&G.

Learning the technical stuff is easy. Learning entrepreneurial thinking is far more difficult, and that's what is most important to us. When they start young, fresh out of college, they haven't been exposed to any other business cultures and don't bring with them bad habits from other companies. They behave as internal entrepreneurs from day-one of their careers.

The Scholars program has been highly successful. We have seen many young leaders grow into impressive responsibilities.

For example, while talking with a bright young engineer working in warehouse operations, I suggested he should try the Finance area. He shyly replied that he didn't know anything about finance. I knew he was very bright, humble, and a life-long learner. I told him not to worry; he would learn the ropes quickly. After just 3 years in financial planning, I offered him the CFO role. Andre Reyes has been a fantastic CFO, transforming the Finance organization and taking results to a whole new level.

> "If somebody offers you an amazing opportunity but you are not sure you can do it, say yes - then learn how to do it later!"
>
> - Richard Branson -

Andre isn't the only one. In fact, we have several leaders under 28 years old who started as Scholars, quickly grew in responsibilities, and now lead significant areas within our company. To name a few:

- Luisa Fajardo, who began her journey with us 11 years ago as a Quality Assurance Scholar, now leads our $100 million Dairy and Food division as its Brand Manager.
- Paulina Gonzalez started 7 years ago as a Scholar in Sales, then became our Brand Manager for Pringles (a brand we represent in Guatemala); she now leads the Powdered Milk business which accounts for $50 million of revenue.
- Jose Luis Quilo, who started 6 years ago as a Scholar in Demand Planning, is now leading Sales to the Traditional Channel (mom-and-pop stores) in Peru.
- Stephan Nolte, who started 5 years ago as a Scholar in the Project Management Office, now leads Sales to the Traditional Channel in Guatemala.
- Jorge Barrientos, who started 8 years ago as a Scholar in Continuous Improvement, now leads Continuous Improvement and Standards in Organizational Engineering.

> "PDC's Scholars Program is one of the most attractive talent pipelines for university students - and one with the highest number of applicants. I feel incredibly proud that PDC attracts such high-potential talent, and that I get to help shape and develop these future leaders."
>
> - Ana Luisa Polanco -
> Trade Marketing Leader, PDC

- Alberto Rebolleda, who started 4 years ago as a Scholar in Distribution Services, is now leading our Commercial Intelligence department.
- Juergen Stolz, who started 8 years ago as a Scholar in the Finance Department, now leads the Liquid Cleaners and Tools category business.
- Mariana Hurtado, who started 2 years ago as a Scholar in the PMO Office, now leads our Conversational Commerce initiatives (embedding chatbots, live chats, messaging, and voice assistants in the online sales process).

I don't worry that we're training these young professionals for other companies. Their experience working within our entrepreneurial culture during their internship has built tremendous loyalty to the company. In fact, Scholars coined the term, "PDC Lovers." That moniker is now widely used throughout PDC. Most of those whom we would like to keep at the end of their internships are enthusiastic about taking permanent jobs with us.

> "Leaders almost always have had opportunities during their twenties and thirties to actually try to lead, to take a risk, and to learn from both triumphs and failures."
>
> - John P. Kotter [30] -

Financial Open Books

With the goal of everybody in the company thinking and acting like an owner, we require everybody to take a basic finance course. We open the books to all our associates. Every month, a volunteer from any area presents our financials for the month and year.

We establish quarterly profit goals. Those goals are then mapped to individual teams, where we empower them to make decisions that will help us achieve our company goals.

When we reach our profit goals, we share part of the profits with everyone. Last year, we shared 14% of the profits with 100% of our associates. This generates a lot of interest in company results at every level.

Figure 13 shows our SIGO mobile app ("Sistema Integral de Gestión Organizacional," our internal enterprise performance model), where all 1,800 associates connect regularly to check our financials, company and team goals, bonuses, and other relevant company news and services.

Figure 13: Our Employee Mobile App

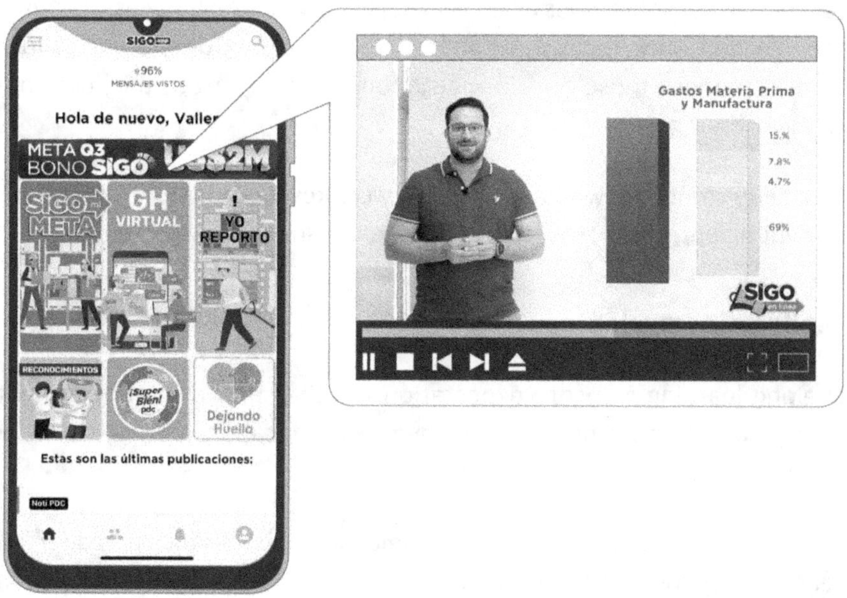

Employee Empowerment

Our organizational design is the biggest contributor to employee engagement. I think the most attractive aspect of our culture, especially to young associates, is the concept of empowerment. Young trainees are given important projects. We are very firm about the quality and the due-date of their deliverables. And we assign a coach to accompany them in the process, ensuring that they are learning while keeping the project risks at an acceptable level.

But here's the key: They are given the authorities they need to accomplish their accountabilities. We manage by results. We do not micromanage what they do (their tasks). Beyond that, they own their time, giving them flexibility in where, when, and how they work.

For instance, we don't track vacation time for our leaders – they have the freedom to take as many days off as they need. Some may take fewer days than expected, while others might take more, depending on their personal and professional circumstances. Life is dynamic, and we recognize that sometimes an extended family vacation is necessary, while at other times, the focus shifts entirely to business. Our approach allows leaders to make these decisions autonomously, as long as they continue to meet their goals.

Flexibility combined with accountability is a key value in our culture. And our young entrepreneurs love the challenge and empowerment.

Leadership Development

Lifelong learning is a core expectation. In the spirit of empowerment, leaders are responsible for their own self-education journey, and the company actively supports them.

Each year, we recommend a curated selection of books for our leadership team and encourage internal book clubs to foster reflection, discussion, and shared growth.

We believe leadership is best developed through experience, not just formal training. At PDC, we challenge our leaders with "stretch" assignments – roles that push them beyond their comfort zones – and surround them with mentorship and real-time feedback to help them grow.

We also rotate high-potential talent across different business lines to broaden their perspective and build enterprisewide knowledge.

I'm proud to say that we now have a great team of leaders at all levels. They accept accountability for results (their products and services). They think and act like entrepreneurs. And they recognize others in the company as internal customers and suppliers.

The PDC senior leadership team

Employee Engagement

In general people are happy. In fact, they're *very* happy!

We conduct a confidential survey every six months to assess how people feel about working in the company. 91% of our 1,800 associates participate in the survey.

A participation rate above 90% is extremely high compared to most companies, which on average have a participation rate between 30% and 40%. Some experts consider a response rate between 50-60% as good, with anything over 70% seen as excellent. [31]

We actually widened the survey some years ago to also include family members; so, today we get a rating from the employee and some family members about how they feel about working in the company.

> "Measuring our Family Happiness Index is a game-changer. It showed me that PDC cares about me not just as an employee, but as a person."
>
> - Ana Luisa Polanco -
> Field Services Leader, PDC

In terms of employee satisfaction, since the transformation, we've consistently received ratings above 80% (Figure 14). And in recent years, we've maintained ratings above 87%. By comparison, the average satisfaction level of employees in the United States, as reported in various surveys, typically ranges between 50% and 65%, depending on the specific metrics and demographics. Achieving anything above 75% is considered very high and very difficult to achieve. [32]

Figure 14: Employee Engagement Results

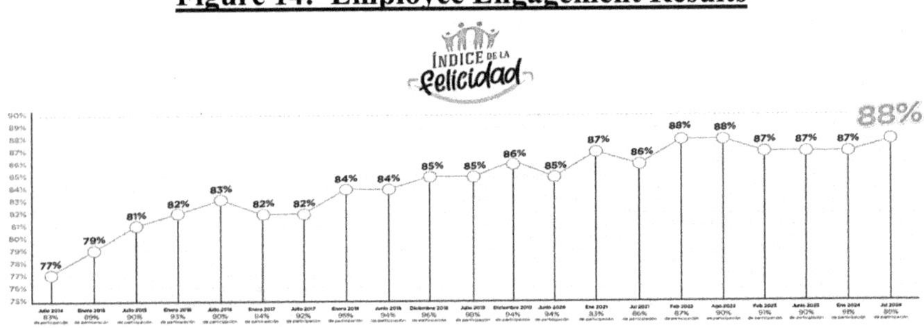

Of course, positive feedback like this feels good, and confirms we've done the right things. But we also take employees' concerns very seriously. We study the results, and sincerely try to understand where we are failing. As a result, we normally initiate 80 to 100 initiatives every semester to close the gaps.

People do leave from time to time, typically for greater compensation. The interesting thing is that, for the past three years, 80% (at the leadership level) ask to come back within the year after they've left. When we ask them why, the answer is simple: They just couldn't, and don't want to, work in a traditional bureaucratic culture.

> "Highly engaged employees make the customer experience.
>
> "Disengaged employees break it."
>
> - Timothy R. Clark -

An email I received from a former employee exemplifies this (edited):

> *"My 5 years working at PDC made a real difference in my professional and personal career. Having worked in two companies since then, I can tell you that PDC is light-years ahead. I'm succeeding in these other companies using what I learned at PDC.*
>
> *"I can also tell you that PDC is special in its human quality – a focus on the well-being of people. That generates real commitment.*
>
> *"PDC is a benchmark in the industry, and is making a difference to so many people. A lot of companies can learn from you. I'm proud to have been a part of PDC, and hope someday (if the opportunity arises) to be able to contribute what I've learned outside back to my PDC family."*
>
> - Luisa García Urzúa

While Luisa has not rejoined us, Ana Luisa Polanco is an example of somebody that we did recruit back. She actually made a podcast, which we distributed to the whole company, about her experience of leaving to join a multinational, and why she was so eager to return to our culture and operating model.

I'll let Ana Luisa tell the story her own way:

> *"[PDC is] a positive work environment where you're genuinely excited to go to work every day.*
>
> *"Our people embody our culture and bring it to life in tangible ways. The level of connectivity among our teams is exceptional. Everyone communicates and works toward a shared objective. We see everything as one single business [and] we understand how our work affects other areas.*
>
> *"They make us partners and ensure we benefit from the company's profits. Having access to the company's and our department's results motivates each of us to identify gaps, improve what we do, and find savings opportunities so we all achieve better outcomes. It helps the entrepreneurial spirit within us. Here, we create, innovate, and grow.*
>
> *"Our leaders support our development, and meritocracy allows us to advance. There's no room for egos or for holding others back.*
>
> *"One of the first comments I received from the El Salvador PDC team during our integration process was: 'It's amazing how you work. You always bring ideas, focus on results; and above all, it's clear that you genuinely enjoy what you do.' That's what happens when teams live the culture, embody the values, and are aligned with our purpose of transforming lives.*
>
> *"The way we operate internally truly sets us apart. So many friends tell you how cool it is to work here. It's not just an image – it is cool to work at PDC."*

- Ana Luisa Polanco
Field Services Leader, PDC

I believe we've attained one of our most important goals: to be the "employer of choice" in all our regions and functions.

13. Example of Benefits: Customers

In addition to financial results and employee engagement, I saw numerous other benefits. One is in our reputation with our customers. We won business we otherwise might not have gotten because we're seen as well run and we deliver results.

We have two types of customers:

- companies that own brands, to which we provide distribution services; and
- retailers to which we sell products (ours and our brand partners').

Brand Companies Who Buy Our Distribution Services

Essity, a Swedish conglomerate and leading global consumer packaged goods (CPG) company, had used our distribution services. They left during our Triage phase, when we were struggling to fix so many problems. When they learned about our new operating model, they came back. Essity is now one of our largest distribution contracts. And the results have been outstanding, growing market share from day one of their return.

Our team successfully managed a Shell Lubricants distribution contract in Guatemala. This led to Shell recognizing us with the prestigious award of their "Best Distributor in Latin America." The accolade was a testament to our innovative organizational model and operational efficiency. Inspired by our proven track record, Shell extended an invitation for us to become their lubricants distributor in Mexico. Our reputation as proficient operators further opened doors to an opportunity to manage Shell's company-owned gas stations and convenience stores in Mexico City. [33]

Another valued brand partner is Otis McAllister, a global market leader in packaged foods with brands including Village Harvest (grains), La Sirena (seafood), and Super Luck Elephant (international flavors of rice). PDC successfully distributed their La Sirena canned tuna and sardine products in Central America before the transformation. They stayed with us through the transformation years, and are well positioned to observe the difference the transformation made to them. Here's what they said:

> *"The inspiring transformation of Grupo PDC resonates with everyone who feels part of this wonderful project. A key pillar of this transformation was the daily drive to become a better version of oneself.*
>
> *"For LA SIRENA, Guatemala represents an example of working with a committed distributor. In the past 10 years, we have doubled sales, strengthened our leadership in the Sardines category, and achieved leadership in the Tuna category.*
>
> *"We hope to continue replicating this same success story, from Guatemala to El Salvador, and soon in Peru. We remain committed to growing with Grupo PDC. I can only thank you for all the dedication in becoming the best distributor in Latin America!"*

- Lorena Ruiz
Sales and Marketing Director LATAM, Otis McAllister

Retailers Who Buy Our Consumer Goods

On the Retailers side, our customers include Walmart, other local retailers (such as the supermarket chain, Unisuper), and traditional mom-and-pop tienditas.

They, too, appreciate our organizational operating model and the results it has delivered. Consider this observation from one of our largest retail customers:

> *"The transformation process of PDC over the past decade has been truly inspiring. Throughout these years, we have witnessed how they have managed to adapt to a constantly changing*

environment, innovating and strengthening their leadership. We have seen their growth, evolution, and extraordinary ability to reinvent themselves, expanding their boundaries both within and beyond the Central American market.

"Their focus on team development, extensive knowledge of the mass consumer market, and close collaboration with business partners have created a solid foundation for sustainable growth and a legacy that will undoubtedly transcend over time.

"It is a great honor for us to be part of this remarkable success story."

- Fredy Gereda
Chairman, Unisuper

Customers don't like surprises; reliability builds trust. Delivering on promises is crucial. We measure fill-rates and Net Promoter Scores (NPS, how likely customers are to recommend your products); these metrics must be at their highest levels.

However, these metrics are the end result of an entire organization delivering on its promises. If any area – manufacturing, logistics, HR, IT, *any* of our 84 functional areas – fails to deliver on their promises to their internal customers, eventually we will disappoint our external customers.

Our customers ultimately evaluate us by our end results. But they also notice how our internal processes ensure that those results can be relied on for years to come. Note this accolade, again from Unisuper:

"From my side, there is nothing left but to congratulate you for modernizing, formalizing, and professionalizing the entire PDC team. Thanks to this and a clear strategic vision, you have achieved an extremely solid CAGR [compound annual growth rate], consolidating yourselves as a strategic business partner for Unisuper.

"I have no doubt that the future will continue to show the fruits of this great work."

- Francisco Mugica
CEO, Unisuper

Of course, our customers (the retailers) will only buy what their customers (consumers) want. Consumer loyalty is critical to our success.

Knowing this, we strive to build a "wide-moat" business. This term, coined by Warren Buffett, describes a company's competitive advantage, which allows it to maintain profitability and market share over an extended period.

Both Buffett and Morningstar have identified several sources of economic moats: [34]

1. **Network effect**: The value of a company's service increases as more people use it (e.g., Facebook, Visa)
2. **Intangible assets**: Patents, brands, and regulatory licenses that prevent competition (e.g., Apple, pharmaceuticals)
3. **Cost advantage**: The ability to provide goods or services at a lower cost than competitors (e.g., Walmart)
4. **Switching costs**: When it's difficult or expensive for customers to switch to a competitor (e.g., ERP solutions)
5. **Efficient scale**: When a company effectively serves a niche market with limited competition (e.g., utility companies)

We strive to build an *Intangibles* moat through our PDC brands. Carlos Penagos, who leads all Brand Managers (and hence all product P&Ls) has an incredible team working to develop "love brands" in all our markets. As described in Chapter 6, this small group of business leaders sources everything internally to create new business lines. Regardless of the category – whether it's dairy products, snack foods, household cleaning chemicals, or any new categories we take on – they build strong brands through their focus on strategy, brand marketing, and effective market distribution.

> "The most important thing to me is figuring out how big a moat there is around the business. What I love, of course, is a big castle and a big moat with piranhas and crocodiles."
>
> - Warren Buffett -

Their focus on their respective markets is the key. They don't have to worry about managing all the support functions they rely on. They trust their internal suppliers to deliver the best of all those diverse specializations.

Today, over 63% of our capital is invested in intangible assets – our leading brands.

The market position of our most important brands in the countries where we operate is shown in Figure 15.

Figure 15: Brand Positions by Country

As you can see, we've done remarkably well. But we have more work to do, both to expand our share of existing markets and to extend our brands to other markets.

I have no doubt we'll achieve both of these goals. A high-performing, empowered, and entrepreneurial organization has been key to delivering the best products and services in our industry to all our customers – brand companies, retailers, and consumers alike.

14. Example of Benefits: Innovation

Product innovation has been explosive, especially considering that just 10 years ago, we had no manufacturing or R&D experience, and no PDC-branded products.

We acquired the P&G Bleach operation for Central America in 2014. At that time, it was producing twelve products. Today we have expanded from a bleach operation to a range of home cleaning solutions, expanding across 150 products and several brands. And we're selling chlorine as an industrial product.

Products at Acquisition

Products Today

This was not an isolated case. For another example, we acquired Australian Dairy. With the leadership of our Dairy Brand Manager, we extended the Australian product line to more than 50 new products in less than three years.

Products at Acquisition

Products Today

Innovation isn't limited to just creating new products. It occurs in all areas in our company from all our empowered entrepreneurs.

For example, David Pardo, who leads our Commercial (sales) organization, came to me last year with a fresh idea on how to improve the efficiency of our sales to mom-and-pop tienditas. This is an important segment to us. Latin America has over 7 million mom-and-pop stores representing over 50% of retail sales. We currently visit over 100,000 of these a week, and get 50% of our revenues from this "Traditional" channel. (The other 50% is from what we call "Modern Trade" – retailers like Walmart and supermarkets.)

However, selling to this channel is extremely costly because of the number of stores, combined with the relatively low average purchase per sales visit. In addition to the cost of selling, delivery costs are high, with many customers scattered throughout remote rural communities.

Digitizing the mom-and-pop channel is on every major CPG (consumer packaged goods) company's agenda. Our IT team looked for a vendor package that would do the job. But after an extensive search, we couldn't find any solutions that would address our challenges. So, we decided to develop the software ourselves.

Understanding the complexity of this, David proposed that we acquire a software engineering company in this space to produce our own commercial (sales) and logistics software. He then designed a solution that would allow freelancers to sell and deliver our products through the regions where we operate. (Think of it like the "DoorDash" or "Uber" of wholesale distribution.)

Today, 100% of our sales to this channel go through this software, and 30% goes through our freelance network. This will extend quickly into new countries where we will have a high presence in mom-and-pops without having direct operations. This solution has dramatically increased coverage while bringing our cost-to-serve down.

These are just a couple examples of many. The interesting thing is that in all these innovation stories, none of the ideas came from me. By empowering these bright leaders across the organization, it is incredible to see creativity and initiative coming from every corner of the enterprise.

15. Example of Benefits: Acquisitions

Early in the implementation of our transformation, we became confident that it gave us the ability to succeed at virtually any strategy. This was not hubris or overconfidence. We had seen the high levels of agility and performance of our organizational operating model.

With our new-found abilities to innovate and execute, we began to think more broadly about the strategic direction of the company.

The distribution business is low margin. It was obvious that the owners of brands were making the bulk of the profits. We wanted to move PDC toward branded consumer goods, a business that would take advantage of our established (and now effective) sales and distribution network.

In 2013, we initially experimented with introducing three brands of our own. To minimize start-up costs, we had them manufactured by third-parties; but we did the marketing, sales, and distribution.

We failed miserably with this initiative. We didn't have sufficient experience with brand creation.

We learned that creating a trusted brand takes significant time and capital. So, we decided that it would be more efficient to buy a leading brand and continue to build on its existing brand equity.

At first, I was skeptical about an acquisitions strategy. After all, most acquisitions tend to lose value for the shareholders. (See Figure 16.)

Figure 16: Most Acquisitions Fail to Deliver Expected Value [35]

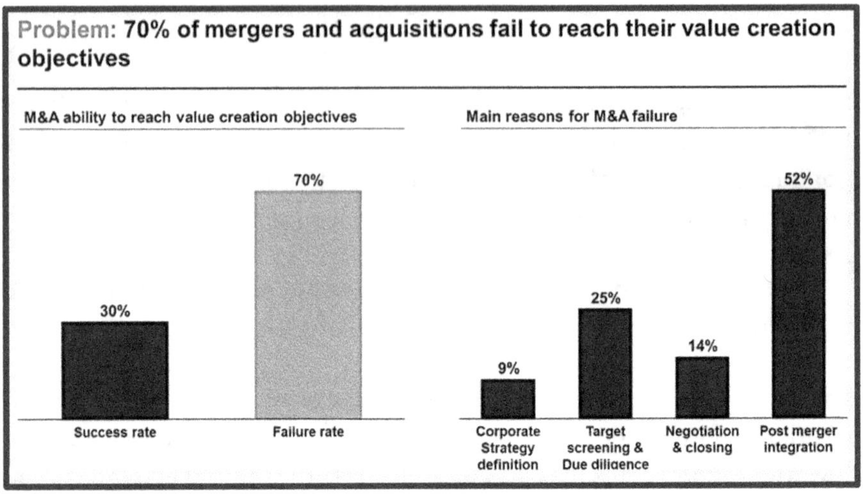

Some companies go on an acquisition spree, buying companies in different industries, because their CEOs are passionate about growing the top line. But from a bottom-line perspective, this doesn't end well in most cases.

Other acquisitions are "bolt-on" in the sense that they expand an existing business. However, the expected synergies are seldom achieved due to slow, incomplete, or failed integrations.

In my experience, in our industry, paying a competitive price for a quality company will normally bring the initial return on capital for the acquisition to around 8%. But when your cost of capital is hovering around 12% and you are hoping for at least a 16% return, you will need to double the earnings to achieve an acceptable return.

The math is quite simple. Imagine that we are evaluating the acquisition of a company that has $50M in sales and $7.5M in EBITDA. Normally this would translate to approximately $4M in Net Operating Profit After Taxes (NOPAT), depending on company-specific depreciation and tax rates.

	Sales	50,000	
	EBITDA	**7,500**	**15%**
	Depreciations	2,500	5%
	Taxes	1,000	2%
	NOPAT	**4,000**	**8%**
	Sales Multiple	1.0x	
	EBITDA Multiple	6.7x	
	Enterprise Value	**50,000**	
	Invested Capital	50,000	
	NOPAT	4,000	
	ROIC (%)	**8.0%**	
	Invested Capital	50,000	
2.0x	NOPAT	8,000	
	ROIC (%)	**16.0%**	

Average multiples for private transactions in our industry within the region are 1.0x sales or 6.7x EBITDA, which would peg the acquisition cost at $50M. This buys us all the assets that will generate future cash flows (fixed assets, working capital, and intangibles like their brands).

Divide the current Net Operating Profit After Tax ($4M) by the invested capital ($50M), and you get an 8% Return on Invested Capital (ROIC).

If we wanted a minimum return of 16%, we would need to double the NOPAT (since you can't reduce the denominator – the invested capital which equals the purchase price paid for the acquisition).

This puts enormous pressure on the acquisition, because from the start you are losing shareholder value. You need to do two things to increase NOPAT and generate a return that would be above the cost of capital and add shareholder value: increase sales, and/or generate operational efficiencies. The path to both these goals is through integration synergies.

In other words, if you are not sure you can double the NOPAT relatively quickly, acquisitions can be a risky strategy. The success of our acquisitions strategy absolutely depended on our ability to achieve full integration quickly. If I wasn't confident that we could do that, we wouldn't have taken the risk.

But as you'll see, our organizational design was the key to seamless, rapid acquisitions integrations.

The First Acquisition: Magia Blanca

Roman philosopher Seneca once said, "Luck is what happens when preparation meets opportunity." Our first acquisition was somewhat serendipitous.

In 2013, I heard that P&G was looking to divest Magia Blanca, the leading bleach brand in Central America with a manufacturing facility in Guatemala. P&G had a best-in-class sodium hypochlorite factory, where they produced and packed twelve different bleach products for Central American markets. The Magia Blanca opportunity presented a way to own a leading brand and market it through our existing distribution capabilities. The potential synergies were clear.

However, the investment bankers who represented P&G in the sale initially did not even want to consider us as a bidder, given that we were a regional company with little acquisition experience. I explained to the sellers at P&G that, yes, we were small; but we were recognized to be one of the best employers in the country. This caught their attention; they wanted to be sure that all their people would be taken care of by the new owner. We went so far as to create a rule that not one person would lose their job because of integration initiatives, a rule we still follow on all acquisitions. This was what got our foot in the door.

The negotiation was led by my brother, Salvador. Despite tough competition, he succeeded in negotiating the purchase. By the end of 2013, we acquired the Magia Blanca brand worldwide (with some minor exceptions), including its main manufacturing facility in Guatemala.

The acquisition came with talented staff who understood the consumer goods industry from the perspective of a multinational consumer-products corporation (P&G). We needed the employees to remain at the company; we needed their expertise in brand building and manufacturing.

PDC's culture and its heavy emphasis on "employees first" was pivotal in facilitating the assimilation. In fact, there was no increase in the attrition rate during the integration.

We selected people from both organizations (the prior PDC and Magia Blanca) into leadership positions based on their competencies. Many former Magia Blanca managers were promoted to Director positions leading shared-services functions (not just bleach) at PDC; others filled needed technical leadership roles. They augmented PDC's talent in areas such as sales, manufacturing, research and development, and quality control. This influx of talent benefitted PDC's existing businesses, as well as Magia Blanca. That was one source of synergies.

The other source of synergies was equally powerful. The Magia Blanca Brand Manager had access to all the capabilities of the entire PDC organization.

In other words, we achieved full, two-way synergies through complete integration.

PDC's organizational operating model and culture of empowerment and entrepreneurship paid off. From 2014 through 2018, the Magia Blanca brand expanded from twelve to more than 100 products, and we grew it geographically from four countries to six. The Home Cleaning business has tripled sales since the acquisition, and now is a $120M business.

Acquisition Number Two: Peru

More serendipity: In late 2018, we heard about a large conglomerate in Peru that was being dismantled and sold as individual units. Dkasa was a home-care brand that had a wide range of cleaning products. It reached a similar consumer to Magia Blanca in the Peruvian market.

It wasn't large, consistently generating about $7M in revenues. And it wasn't growing. To the seller, it was insignificant. Thus, we were able to get a good deal. The acquisition closed in 2019.

Once we acquired Dkasa, we found it had a poor management structure that lacked clear accountabilities, and employee engagement was quite low. Many employees were displeased with their existing compensation and benefits, and didn't enjoy the work environment at the company. Clearly, this was a company that had been neglected within a larger conglomerate structure.

We had to let go of poor performers in upper management. But we were able to retain many great people. Retention was high, I believe, because employees appreciated our culture and our disciplined leadership. In the first year, the attrition rate of the company was cut by nearly 50%.

Again, synergies drove our thinking. By giving Dkasa access to all the capabilities of PDC's shared services, we were able to grow the acquired business quickly and dramatically in Peru. Sales have grown from $7M to $40M in 5 years (41.6% annual sales growth rate, which includes a second acquisition in the country).

Synergies worked the other way as well; the acquisition improved the performance of our other brands. Dkasa gave the full spectrum of PDC brands entry into the Peruvian market, with a fully functioning production facility, distribution operations, and a sales force that reached wholesalers, mom-and-pop stores, and supermarkets in Peru. And we learned some manufacturing technologies and processes that were new to us.

Acquisition Number Three: Milk

Australian Dairy was a family-owned and well recognized dairy brand operating in El Salvador and Guatemala. Its products included whole milk powder and ultra-high-temperature processed (UHT) liquid milk.

Powdered milk is a staple in Latin America owing to low prices and longer shelf life in areas where refrigeration is scarce or unaffordable. By 2020, Australian Dairy had become the biggest powdered-milk brand in El Salvador, with around 55% of the market share. Small grocery and mom-and-pop retailers preferred it over its main competitor, the multinational Nestle.

In Guatemala, the company had only reached a 14% market share.

The good news was that it had good cash flow and a high ROA. It also had a well-run packaging facility in Guatemala City that could be expanded to increase its capacity – creating additional potential synergies for us.

The price the owners demanded was high; and a good portion of it was goodwill. To recuperate the cost of this acquisition, profits would have to double in the next five years. Again, it all came down to the synergies we expected to gain.

And, of course, synergies depended on full integration with PDC's structure and operating model.

This was a big acquisition for us, given that Australian had about the same EBITDA as all of PDC at the time. Australian had nearly 550 employees, and PDC approximately 1,500; the acquisition increased PDC's staff size by 35%.

Adding to the integration challenge, the culture at Australian was quite different from ours. When we first visited them, our Brand Managers leader, Carlos Panagos, remarked, "Everyone above a certain level has an office and a secretary. That's just not how we do business!" In contrast, we have open offices (even for executives).

But we followed our now-tested playbook (which I'll describe shortly), and the integration went smoothly.

We were able to double sales in just three years (Figure 17). We now have 68.8% market share in El Salvador, and 33.5% in Guatemala (from the number 7 brand to number 2 in three years). The acquired company flourished as it assimilated the PDC culture and was "plugged into" the PDC organizational operating model.

<u>Figure 17: Growth in the Australian Dairy Business</u>

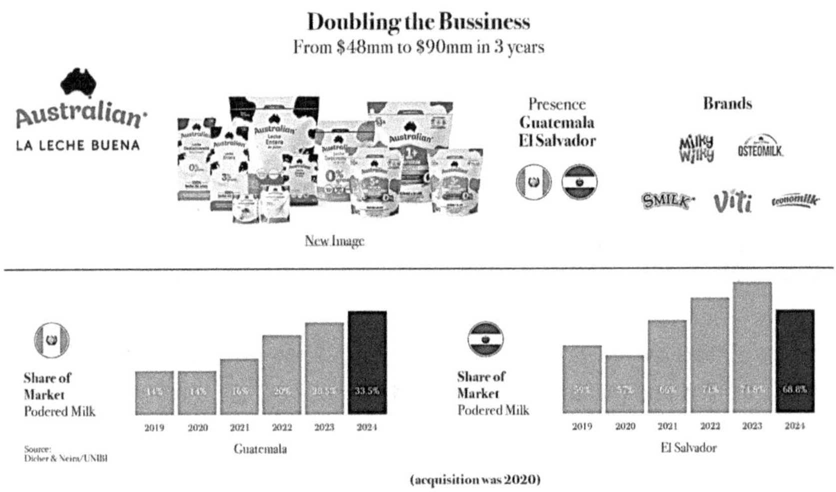

Again, the synergies worked in both directions. For example, we were able to transition existing Magia Blanca products from a third-party distributor in El Salvador to our newly acquired distribution network. Sales increased dramatically.

It's funny.... A university professor predicted this acquisition would fail and would bankrupt our company. He cited loss of focus, since in his mind, the Dairy category was not a core strength.

It seems that he missed the point. What this professor didn't understand was that we'd designed an organization that could pursue multiple categories in multiple markets simultaneously, all drawing on shared competencies in all the functions – marketing, sales, production, packaging, warehousing, transportation, and all the business services.

In fact, our core strength is not our current product lines. It's developing leading brands across multiple categories, without having to replicate all those support functions. It's founded on our fully integrated organizational operating model.

The results show how wrong that professor was. We hit our seven-year financial targets (which we had presented to the bank which financed the purchase) in just three years.

> PDC's core strength is really our integrated organizational operating model.

How We Do Integration

Integrating an acquisition while leaving a CEO in place would have been impossible. Instead, we integrate all areas of the acquired company with our existing shared services. (This, of course, eliminates the need for a CEO of the acquisition, just as we don't need CEOs by country or business.)

On the day we closed the Australian acquisition, the owner/CEO asked me who was going to lead the company locally. I replied, "nobody." He was furious, said this would never work, and threatened to cancel the deal. I calmed him down and convinced him that this would be to the benefit of his brand and his people.

The integration worked seamlessly; and as I said above, was very successful. (Sadly, due to COVID, the previous owner/CEO did not live to see his legacy prosper.)

Our structure makes acquisitions integration much easier. In fact, it's quite simple....

First, we analyze the acquired company's organization chart in terms of the internal lines of business in each group. Most of their functions map directly into our shared services. And the acquired brand-management functions (very few) become a new position (or group) within our brand-management group.

This gives us two-way synergies.

Each acquisition brought us a new brand – and a new Brand Manager. Since everything else is a shared service, that Brand Manager has access to all the rich depth of our entire organization.

In parallel, each acquisition brought in new talent with new skills and perspectives, as well as new assets (infrastructure). Integrated into our shared-services, these made all our internal lines of business stronger for preexisting as well as the acquired brands.

The key to making this work is the business-within-a-business operating model. All our internal entrepreneurs are eager to please their internal customers. We have well-established processes for linking all our Brand Managers to the services they need, from marketing and sales through production and distribution. Everything meshes.

This organizational design, which is the source of our synergies, also speeds acquisition integration. We achieve full integration in just *three to six months*. This stands in stark contrast to conventional wisdom, which says synergies take two to three years to materialize.

The acquisition deal is driven by a team led by my brother, Salvador. They have a very disciplined process of analyzing, prospecting, negotiating, and closing acquisitions.

Even before the deal is closed, the acquisition integration process begins. That is led by our Organizational Engineering team, since it requires their in-depth expertise in our structure and operating model.

Acquisitions have been a significant driver of our growth to date. In less than a decade, we have shifted from having 0% of our total revenue generated by PDC-owned brands to approximately 60%. When measured by gross profit, PDC brands now contribute nearly 80%. There is no doubt that acquisitions will continue to be a central part of our growth strategy.

16. Example of Benefits: External Sale of Support Services

As our entrepreneurial culture evolved throughout every function in the organization, numerous leaders started asking me if they could sell their products or services not only to their internal customers but to external customers as well.

After careful consideration, we concluded that every group could sell to external customers if and only if:

A. External sales will not affect the level of service to internal customers.
B. We do not sell to the competition anything which would impair our core strategy or competitive advantage.

After these rules were communicated, several entrepreneurs energetically started to grow their businesses outside the company, including:

- Software sales
- HR services
- Promotional services
- Digital marketing services

As I mentioned in Chapter 14, David Pardo (head of Commercial, i.e., sales) had an idea of how to significantly improve the complex sales and logistics processes by which we service the mom-and-pop channel. As it turns out, a lot of consumer goods companies in Latin America had this same problem. Oscar Mejia, who leads Shared Services including IT, is now selling our software to other distributors and consumer packaged goods (CPG) companies who don't compete with our products. And he is in conversations with several ERP software vendors who want to certify and integrate our solution with their software for the CPG industry.

Human Resources (HR) services have grown and matured inside PDC, including recruiting, employee engagement surveys, and payroll services, among others. Multinational CPG companies that we distribute have employees in our regions, and some of them now buy our HR services. We are currently selling about $1M per year in HR services.

Because of our geographic reach, we have a big Field Services team that helps with product placement and promotions. So, our Field Services leader, Ana Luisa Polanco, now offers promotional services to other consumer goods companies.

As part of our transformation, we have acquired companies that previously operated as stand-alone businesses but are now integrated into PDC as internal functions. Notably, we acquired a software company and an advertising agency. Both were already in the business of serving external customers. Today, they are fully integrated and PDC has become one of their key clients; but they continue to sell to external clients and to manage their own P&Ls.

Integration with PDC not only benefited PDC. It enhanced their external businesses as well.

With the addition of PDC's business, their larger groups permitted deeper specialization and it expanded career opportunities. For instance, our in-house digital marketing team joined forces with the advertising agency, which now includes over 110 professionals. This integration has not only elevated our internal capabilities but also preserved the entrepreneurial spirit of these companies.

Furthermore, by becoming part of a larger enterprise, they now benefit from shared services in areas like IT, HR, planning, and finance, freeing them to focus more on their core competencies and growth.

Software, HR Services, Promotional Services, and Digital Marketing have been big successes. This is remarkable given the typically high failure rate when launching a business from scratch (Figure 18).

Figure 18: The Difficulty of Starting New Businesses [36]

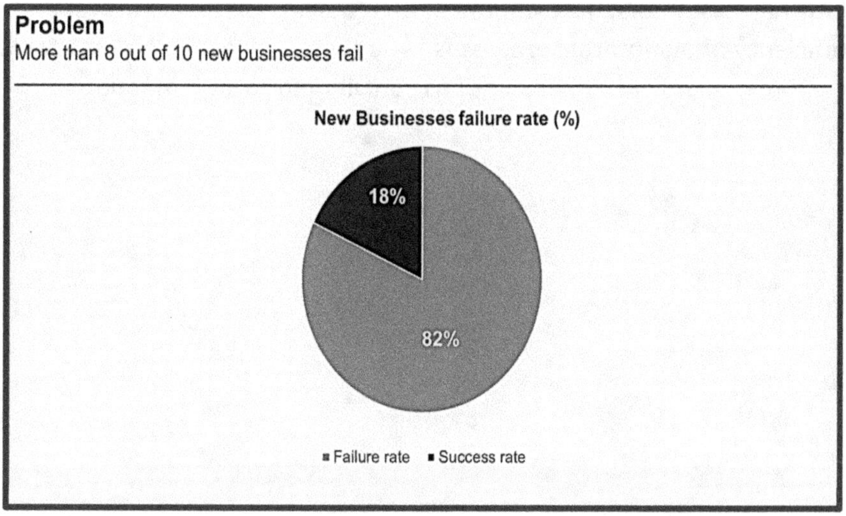

New lines of business, arising from what were formerly just internal service providers, are currently contributing 5% of Gross Profits. At their current growth rate, these new businesses should amount to 10% of total Gross Profits within the next three years.

Furthermore, these additional sales absorb some indirect costs. Economies of scale bring the costs of internal services down. This contributes to profits in all our businesses.

But as Oscar Mejia points out, the profits (small in the greater context of company earnings) are not the real benefit. More important is that our internal entrepreneurs are learning what it takes to compete in the real market, honing their entrepreneurial skills. They then bring that entrepreneurial excellence to their internal customers.

> "Competing in the real world has improved the quality of teamwork and the efficiency of our internal processes.
>
> "And the positive impacts on internal customer-supplier relationships has contributed to staff morale."
>
> \- Oscar Mejía-
> Business Services Leader, PDC

Having people understand how to treat customers, including peers as internal customers, has improved the quality of teamwork and the efficiency of our internal processes. And the positive impacts on internal customer-supplier relationships has contributed to staff morale.

17. Example of Benefits: Reputation

As the transformation bears fruit, people are beginning to notice. Even critics have shifted their perspective. Today, PDC is celebrated not just for its strong financial performance and growth, but also for its exceptional operational excellence and employee engagement.

I'm honored that we constantly get requests from other companies to visit us and learn about our organizational operating model.

Although we did not transform our organization for the sake of our reputation, the fact that our reputation has been enhanced has yielded additional tangible returns.

Reputation with Our Banks

Here's an example:

We have excellent relationships with our banks. We have developed a great deal of trust as we consistently under-promise and over-deliver. We share our financial statements openly, including whatever challenges we may be facing. Of course, we have been very consistent and reliable in servicing our credit obligations.

As a result, over the course of the past few years, our banks have supported us by financing four new acquisitions.

> "Bam Guatemala, an affiliate of Bancolombia, partnered with PDC as a lead structuring agent of a unique acquisition funding facility to fuel its growth, largely because of PDC's commitment to integrity and an unparalleled reputation for operational excellence."
>
> - Federico Bolaños -
> *General Manager, Bam Guatemala*

Trust has led to better terms, including: temporary waivers to leverage caps (our debt-to-EBITDA ratio); better interest rates than the prevailing market rates; and more lenient amortization schedules.

Reputation with Acquisition Targets

Another really valuable benefit has been the reputation we have earned as a "preferred buyer" of businesses.

As I said, acquisitions have become a central part of our growth strategy. However, some sellers are hesitant to sell their "babies." And many have concerns that are unrelated to acquisition price, such as our ability to quickly expand their legacies while taking good care of their brands and their people – in many cases, friends they've worked with for a long time.

That's where reputation comes into play. PDC can point to its successful acquisitions track record, and the genuine happiness of the integrated teams.

Unlike family businesses, big multinationals look for buyers that make their job as sellers easier. They like the fact that we will take all their people, and are very agile in the decision making and integration process. For example, after they sold us Magia Blanca, P&G cited us as one of their best divestitures based on the ease and speed with which we integrated their people into our company. In fact, P&G has invited us to participate in three additional bids after Magia Blanca.

> "The Magia Blanca transaction was one of the most memorable that I have worked on, given the professionalism, agility, and fair-mindedness of the PDC team."
>
> - Mario Christoforou -
> Former Global Head of Corporate M&A, Procter & Gamble

Sellers have come to know this, and our reputation has brought us opportunities and given us an additional tool during negotiations. Competing bidders generally include Private Equity firms and other strategic buyers like us – most of whom have built the opposite reputation for themselves, known for their aggressive cost-cutting efforts and lack of concern for the wellbeing of the acquired teams or brands.

During a recent negotiation, the executive representing a seller compared us to an existing offer from a Private Equity firm. We could not meet their bid, given our pricing discipline. However, we could promise to take much better care of the executive and her entire team. We offered an entrepreneurial culture where her team would now be empowered to grow the business by leveraging the rest of PDC's capabilities and organizational systems. These were powerful sources of differentiation in the competitive M&A space, and put us at the top of their list of future buyers.

Reputation with Others

As described in Chapter 12, we have a reputation as a great place to work. That has helped us attract top talent, even when we can't afford to pay top dollar (as companies that are not great places to work must).

While somewhat less tangible, our reputation for organizational excellence, along with our innovative organizational design, has attracted attention from other CEOs globally. That's led to speaking opportunities and valuable connections (networking).

In all, I consider our reputation for operational excellence and for being an employer of choice to be an incredibly valuable intangible asset.

18. Where We Are Now

As I reflect on where we came from and where we are, I must say that I'm very pleased with the results of our investment in transformation. We are far from done. But we've accomplished quite a lot.

Organizational Excellence

Dean offers an "organizational excellence self-assessment for executives" which defines, in just ten words, what the goal is in organizational design. [37] I'll use that framework to review where we are, quoting his definitions (in italics) followed by my assessment.

Scalability

"Your organization can grow in size and/or diversification, indefinitely, without any material changes in its organizational operating model."

We have assigned every internal line of business that we need, now and as far as we can see into the future, to someone in our organization. As we grow in size, some lines of business may subdivide into multiple groups. And as we diversify, we may add new Brand Managers. We can do this without any change in the overall operating model.

Agility

"To prosper in this VUCA world, your organization can rapidly reconfigure its capabilities to address new challenges and opportunities, without any material changes in its organizational operating model."

Walk-throughs allow us to quickly assemble all the right specialists from anywhere in the company to address new challenges – both problems and opportunities. And any internal line of business can be involved in multiple walk-throughs (initiatives) at any point in time. New strategies or crises require a new walk-through, not a change in our structure.

Stability

"The organization can adapt to changes – including people changing jobs, technology innovations, and new methods – without any material changes in its organizational operating model."

Because we designed our structure based on principles, not personalities, as people come and go, or rotate in the course of their careers with us, there is no need for any change in structure. And all our internal entrepreneurs continually seek new technologies and methods to improve their businesses within the business. Again, as this occurs, there's no fundamental change in our operating model.

Innovation

"Innovation is not constrained to a small group ("innovation" or R&D group), which creates a bottleneck for innovation, deprives everyone else of growth opportunities, and wastes so much talent. Instead, innovation is everywhere, at two levels: 1) innovation in the way each group operates (its products/services, skills, tools, methods, and processes); and 2) the delivery of innovations that contribute to enterprise strategies."

Every group is a business within a business. Our internal entrepreneurs all continually innovate within their lines of business. And they all contribute to enterprise innovations, like strategic initiatives, through walk-throughs.

Acquisition integration

"Once the deal is done, acquisition integration occurs quickly (months, not years), and achieves all the promised two-way synergies – the acquired business (e.g., product line) benefits from the depth of capabilities (all support services) throughout the enterprise; and the entire enterprise benefits from the acquired capabilities (its talent and support services)."

As described in Chapter 15, we are able to achieve full two-way synergies through complete integration of acquisitions in just three to six months.

Domains

"Across the organization, there are no overlapping accountabilities for functions (no internal competition and territorial battles) and there are no gaps (missing capabilities)."

Every group has a written domain statement that describes its boundaries in terms of what business it's in – what it sells. There are no overlaps or internal competition. And while we may have some gaps, we fill them (following the principles) once we identify the need.

Teamwork

"There's a lot more to teamwork than good interpersonal relations (trust, communications, etc.). Cross-boundary teams form dynamically (not fixed processes, except where appropriate). Teams form laterally (not requiring people to work up and back down the hierarchy). For every project/service, one group is accountable for the entire deliverable. Others on the team are clear about their individual accountabilities for sub-deliverables (results, not functions/tasks/processes). Priorities are aligned such that all team members have time to contribute expected results."

We use the walk-through methodology (Chapter 10) to form teams for new projects and services. Teams are self-forming and self-managing. The membership in each team is tailored to the needs of each unique project or service. We know the single point of accountability for the entire project/service (the prime contractor), and what deliverables each subcontractor is to contribute. And groups contribute to multiple project/service teams at the same time.

Specialization

"High levels of individual performance require specialization. Specialists always outperform generalists in their field of study. In fact, specialization is the very reason organizations exist; an organization of generalists performs no better than an equal number of individuals. As long as it's good at teamwork, the more an organization permits specialization, the greater its potential performance. Consolidation of shared services optimizes specialization; there's no need for siloed business units or decentralization (e.g., self-sufficient business units, country managers), which reduce specialization."

We have optimized specialization by making *everything* a shared service.

Empowerment

"Empowerment means that authorities and accountabilities match. If the organizational design separates authorities from accountabilities, then (using black-and-white language to make the point) the group with authorities becomes an unconstrained tyrant (no checks and balances); while the group with accountabilities cannot get their job done and becomes a scapegoat when the decisions of the group with authority fail. A healthy organizational design systematically matches authorities and accountabilities."

This is one of the two Pillars at the core of our organizational design. Customers decide what to buy from internal suppliers. But suppliers are empowered to deliver their products and services in the best way they know how. Bosses hold staff accountable for results (which are clearly defined in walk-throughs), but don't micromanage them. And staff have the time and resources they need to deliver their commitments.

Engagement

"Employee engagement depends on more than just a great boss. It's founded on a supportive and inspiring work environment. Expectations

are feasible, not unreasonable. The culture is supportive. Metrics are controllable and fair. Everybody has growth opportunities. And critically important, everybody feels a sense of purpose. Purpose means using one's unique talents to do something hard (that they'll be proud of) and that has value to others."

Our employee engagement scores (Chapter 12) testify that PDC is a great place to work. And in addition to our "people first" culture, everybody has a sense of purpose – delivering valued products and services to their internal and external customers.

More To Do

As successful as the PDC transformation has been so far, let me be the first to say that we have more to do.

We have to ensure that walk-throughs (the team-formation process described in Chapter 10) are reliably done at the start of every project. I'm afraid that some of our people still skip this step (and their projects inevitably suffer).

We're continuing to work on our culture, expanding it to include behavioral principles that operationalize all of our values.

We've learned that managing-by-results (the essence of Pillar Two, empowerment) is no easy task – it requires a rigorous and well-structured performance evaluation system. We're proud of our systems of accountability. But we have more to do on metrics, for example, measures of entrepreneurship such as internal customer relationships, competitive costs, innovation, and planning for the future.

And we have work to do on the internal economy. We are able to view P&Ls by major department; but we need to take that down to the small-group level. We need to learn to plan budgets based on what people are expected to *deliver* (projects and services across the enterprise, termed "investment-based budgeting"), not what they plan to spend within their individual groups. We need to do a better job of incorporating all indirect costs (including the cost of internal services bought from other groups) into each group's rates.

And we need a dynamic enterprise priority-setting process so that we can realign our resources quickly as strategies shift – one that ensures that, for each new initiative, prime contractors and subcontractors (everybody in the walk-through) all have the resources they need to deliver their respective shares of the project.

Impacts on My Role as CEO

Yes, we have more to do. Organizational excellence is not a project, once and done; it's a long-term commitment to working "on the machine."

But in general, our organization is working extremely well.

As a result, I rarely get dragged into day-to-day issues. In fact, I'm amazed at how much gets done without me!

I've been able to shift my focus to more impactful uses of my time: nurturing our leadership talent, consistently reinforcing and evolving our operating model and culture at every level, and exploring strategic opportunities.

> "Great leaders are not cogs *in* the machine.
>
> "They're designers *of* the machine."
>
> - N. Dean Meyer -

On a personal note, I now enjoy my role more than ever. Constantly fighting fires, or pushing the organization to get things done, was very draining. I get my energy from thinking about strategic issues, and from helping people succeed within our company. Now, for the most part, that's what I do.

Our transformation has not only delivered results for shareholders. It's made PDC a great place to work for all our staff, including me!

19. Words to the Wise

I've learned quite a lot about the science of organizational design in the course of our transformation. And I'm continually learning more.

As I reflect on our journey, I draw a few conclusions that may be of some small value to other leaders.

Make Organizational Excellence Your Top Priority

First and foremost, great leaders don't just work *IN* the machine; they work *ON* the machine. Organizational design is one of the most fundamental responsibilities, and competencies, of leadership.

The most important advice I could give to my peers is to consider organizational excellence their *most* strategic initiative. It leverages everything that you, and everything everybody else does, too.

> "The most important job of a leader is to design an organization in which everyone can succeed, with or without her."
>
> - N. Dean Meyer -

And this is an investment that pays off year after year. A company operating under the correct organizational design will significantly outperform its competitors.

When to Address Organizational Design

Don't delay! The sooner, the better.

Transformation gets more complex if a business has already scaled. If you have an organization that's divided into siloed business units, be forewarned that untangling these "kingdoms" once they have been established, while necessary, can be painful.

It's not just that it's easier when you're small. The correct organizational design will improve every aspect of organizational performance. It defines clear boundaries, induces great teamwork, enhances morale, and develops everybody's entrepreneurial skills.

In other words, designing an organization that can scale will create the engine that drives growth. That's why this subject is crucial for entrepreneurs who are just starting out, as well as those at later stages of growth.

> Designing an organization that can scale will create the engine that drives growth.

When speaking with entrepreneurs leading small, early-stage companies, they often tell me that they can't fund all the boxes (shared-services functions) required for a full-scale organization; and they're right. However, they can design the optimal organization of the future, and then put the same name in several boxes until growth permits additional leadership headcount. After all, somebody must be accountable for everything that is happening and should be happening in the future, even if you're small.

Doing this not only clarifies accountabilities for current business initiatives. Perhaps more importantly, it clarifies who's accountable for thinking of all the things you're not currently thinking about.

And it provides a clear growth path as you scale, as in, "Now is the time to fill this box with a leader who's a real specialist."

Yes, it's easier when you're small, and the investment pays off over a longer period. But, it's never too late. These principles and change processes can be applied to organizations of any size, and in any industry.

Stick to the Plan

I have to admit, not all our new ventures have been successful. While our organizational model has enabled extraordinary growth and innovation, we encountered significant challenges whenever we deviated from it.

In several instances, I made the mistake of launching new ventures outside of our established structure, in keeping with the notion of an "incubator." For example, we acquired two small software companies in the hope of building an e-commerce supermarket. That venture failed. My biggest mistake was leaving this business as a separate business unit – a "silo."

These new businesses operated with decentralized support functions that lacked the maturity, specialization, and scale of our internal shared services. The learning curve to bring these decentralized functions up to the standards of our integrated organization was far longer and steeper than we had anticipated. Specialized expertise could not be developed quickly or cost-effectively in these small stand-alone units.

In contrast, within PDC, the accumulated scale of our internal functions allows for deep specialization, driving higher quality, innovation, and cost-efficiency. These internal capabilities are the product of decades of continuous improvement, professional focus, and innovation. Rebuilding that level of expertise from scratch in isolated ventures is not only costly but nearly impossible within reasonable timeframes.

To make matters worse, its leaders were not well integrated into our culture.

Without access to our ecosystem of entrepreneurial internal suppliers and our culture and systems of accountability, these ventures struggled to achieve excellence – and as a result, all of them ultimately failed.

I had neglected the most important lesson from our prior acquisitions: The key to our success in acquisitions as a growth strategy is complete and rapid integration. The same is true of new ventures.

Ultimately, we learned that it is far more efficient, scalable, and reliable to build new businesses by plugging them into the integrated organization, and then assembling all the required services from our existing functions.

Today, we are very disciplined about this lesson. Every new venture is architected within the organizational structure we have built. We no longer attempt to create standalone units. Instead, we leverage the strength of our integrated entrepreneurial organization, ensuring that every new initiative benefits from the scale, specialization, and excellence that our structure provides.

The Importance of Humility

The next reflection I'd like to share with you is more personal. It has to do with your attitude as a leader.

In too many cases, CEOs (and other senior leaders) think they can do all this themselves.

There's hubris in thinking that their intuition is as good as science, or that their experience leading companies (however successfully) is equivalent to the experience of an individual who has dedicated his life to understanding organizational design.

The problem is not just that these CEOs lack depth in the science of organizational design. Their intuition leads them to designs which are based on their past experiences – traditional designs that haven't worked well for many decades. This is not the path to a breakthrough!

> "It ain't what you don't know that gets you into trouble.
>
> "It's what you know for sure that ain't so."
>
> \- Josh Billings -

Wise executives are life-long learners. They don't pretend to know it all. They know what they do know, and are humble about their limits.

I can honestly say that we would not have been able to do this without Dean's vision, theory, implementation and change-management processes, and guidance.

I advise my peers to take the science of organizational design seriously, and to demonstrate their strength through humility – through a willingness to reach out for help from the experts, via their writings and in person.

Invest!

Our entrepreneurial operating model is a precious asset. Like our customers' loyalty to our brands, it's another form of "moat" that competitors cannot easily replicate without years of transformational work.

And we all know that valued assets are never free. It took a significant investment of thought, time, and money. This is certainly not an overnight success story.

Our profitability dropped during the first two years of the transformation, with leadership's (and my own) attention focused on the change processes. Despite the business pressures, I made sure everyone knew that it was our top strategic priority, more important than short-term financial results.

And our investment is not one-time. There are ongoing costs.

We have a dedicated Organizational Engineering (OE) team which we created at the beginning of the transformation process. It's led by a senior executive who reports directly to me.

Reporting to the head of Organizational Engineering, we currently have four dedicated organizational engineers. They are continually fine-tuning different components of the organization. They facilitate change in all five organizational systems: structure, internal economy, culture, processes, and metrics. In addition, they provide other internal consultancies, including facilitating walk-throughs and strategic planning.

Note that assigning such a senior leader to OE, as well as the several organizational engineers that work in this area, is another indication of the strategic value of our organizational operating model, and of how high the return on this investment has been and will continue to be.

I know that many companies assign some of these functions to Human Resources. However, managing talent (HR) is very different from engineering the organizational ecosystem. HR deals with the individual and the employment relationship, while OE deals with organizational systems. HR prefers stability, while OE is transformational. I strongly recommend that OE be established separately from HR.

The Bottom Line

Yes, every precious asset requires investment.

But now, we are reaping the benefits in every aspect of our business.

Our operating model allows us to extend our current businesses in many ways – new products, new geographies, and new methods and technologies in every function. Every aspect of our organizational design is infinitely scalable.

Our operating model allows us to continually, and rapidly, adapt to ever-changing business environments. It gives us real agility in our business strategies.

We use our operating model to supercharge acquisitions with our ability to quickly realize the maximum in two-way synergies and make those deals orders-of -magnitude more successful.

In every function – not just our consumer products and distribution services, but all our internal products and services as well, at every level – we are continually innovating and planning our future, and optimizing our processes, our tools, and our thinking.

And it not only significantly improves our performance. Our distinctive corporate structure and culture serve as a powerful source of long-term competitive advantage, positioning us to maintain market leadership and to drive sustainable growth into the future. This, combined with the competitive advantage of our renowned brands, has created a "wide moat." These two intangible assets, meticulously developed over time, present a formidable challenge for competitors to replicate.

Transformation is an investment that will continue to pay off in so many ways. Our organizational design is built to last. It houses us in a solid fortress that will benefit our people, our customers, our shareholders, and our communities for decades to come. It has transformed lives, and created a legacy that I hope will endure for generations.

I can honestly say that the time and money we put into our organizational operating model was the best investment we've ever made.

Endnotes

1. Theodore Seuss Geisel.

2. https://www.linkedin.com/posts/dave-snowden-2a93b_it-is-a-truth-that-should-be-universally-activity-7092085309923831809-HGs1/. 2024.

3. Meyer, N. Dean. *Principle-based Organizational Structure.* Danbury, CT: NDMA Publishing. 2017.

4. Meyer, N. Dean. *How Organizations Should Work.* Danbury, CT: NDMA Publishing. 2022.

5. Ackoff, Russell. "The Learning and Legacy of Dr. W. Edwards Deming." Event hosted by Clare Crawford-Mason and Lloyd Dobyns. 1994.

6. Source: N. Dean Meyer.

7. Meyer, N. Dean. *How Organizations Should Work.* Danbury, CT: NDMA Publishing. 2022. Page 342.

8. Meyer, N. Dean. *How Organizations Should Work.* Danbury, CT: NDMA Publishing. 2022. Page 47.

9. https://getfrankli.com/knowledge-centre/connecting-employee-engagement-and-performance

   https://firstup.io/blog/employee-engagement-key-to-company-success/

10. https://getfrankli.com/knowledge-centre/connecting-employee-engagement-and-performance

11. https://getfrankli.com/knowledge-centre/connecting-employee-engagement-and-performance

12. https://getfrankli.com/knowledge-centre/connecting-employee-engagement-and-performance

    https://engagedly.com/blog/impact-of-employee-engagement-on-productivity/

13. https://www.gallup.com/workplace/321725/gallup-q12-meta-analysis-report.aspx

14. https://www.gallup.com/workplace/321725/gallup-q12-meta-analysis-report.aspx

15. https://www.gallup.com/workplace/321725/gallup-q12-meta-analysis-report.aspx

16. https://getfrankli.com/knowledge-centre/connecting-employee-engagement-and-performance

    https://www.gallup.com/workplace/321725/gallup-q12-meta-analysis-report.aspx

17. https://getfrankli.com/knowledge-centre/connecting-employee-engagement-and-performance
    https://firstup.io/blog/employee-engagement-key-to-company-success/

18. https://www.linkedin.com/pulse/impact-employee-engagement-productivity-techplay

https://blog.clearcompany.com/employee-engagment-impacts-performance-and-productivity

https://business.talkspace.com/articles/impact-of-employee-engagement-on-productivity

https://www.employment-studies.co.uk/system/files/resources/files/469.pdf

19. Collins, Jim. *Turning the Flywheel: A Monograph to Accompany Good to Great.* Random House Business. February, 2019.

20. https://www.tugboatinstitute.com/what-is-evergreen/

21. Derived from: Meyer, N. Dean. *How Organizations Should Work.* Danbury, CT: NDMA Publishing. 2022. Part 3, and page 271.

22. Meyer, N. Dean. *How Organizations Should Work.* Danbury, CT: NDMA Publishing. 2022. Page 124.

23. Chandler, Alfred D. *Strategy and Structure.* Cambridge, MA: The MIT Press. 1962.

24. Meyer, N. Dean. *How Organizations Should Work.* Danbury, CT: NDMA Publishing. 2022. Page 63.

25. Ackoff, Russell. "The Learning and Legacy of Dr. W. Edwards Deming." Event hosted by Clare Crawford-Mason and Lloyd Dobyns. 1994.

26. Meyer, N. Dean. *How Organizations Should Work.* Danbury, CT: NDMA Publishing. 2022. Page 73.

27. Meyer, N. Dean. *How Organizations Should Work.* Danbury, CT: NDMA Publishing. 2022. Page 77.

28. Meyer, N. Dean. *How Organizations Should Work.* Danbury, CT: NDMA Publishing. 2022. Page 78.

29. JPMorgan Chase 2024 Annual Report, Letter to Shareholders.

30. Harvard Business Review. May-June, 1990. Page 109.

31. https://www.culturemonkey.io/guides/measuring-employee-engagement/challenges-in-measuring-employee-engagement/impact-of-survey-participation-rate-in-measuring-engagement/

https://peoplepulse.com/resources/useful-articles/survey-response-rates/

https://www.linkedin.com/pulse/what-typical-employee-survey-response-rate-how-do-i-increase-bye

32. https://www.cnn.com/2023/05/11/success/employee-job-satisfaction-survey-conference-board/index.html

https://elearningindustry.com/job-satisfaction-statistics-key-data-and-insights

https://www.pewresearch.org/social-trends/2024/12/10/job-satisfaction/

33. During a subsequent strategic planning session, we reflected on our core strengths and market opportunities. With a unanimous decision to sharpen our focus on the consumer goods sector, we have since strategically divested all operations associated with Shell.

34. https://www.morningstar.com/investing-definitions/economic-moat

https://en.wikipedia.org/wiki/Economic_moat

35. Source: Domont Consulting.

36. Source: Domont Consulting.

37. https://www.ndma.com/orgexcellence

Biography: Sergio Paiz

Sergio Paiz is the CEO of Grupo PDC, a multi-business company with a regional presence from Mexico to Peru. PDC manufactures and distributes consumer products to retailers ranging from Walmart to more than 100,000 mom-and-pop neighborhood stores. With PDC's empowered, entrepreneurial organization, Sergio's personal focus is on business strategy, acquisitions, and organizational transformation.

Prior to this role, Sergio co-founded several start-ups.

Sergio holds a degree in Industrial and Manufacturing Systems Engineering from Lehigh University, and has completed executive education programs at Harvard. He's an active member of YPO and a former finance professor at Universidad Francisco Marroquín.

Sergio has also served as an external board member of Interbanco (a nationwide bank), CIBUS (McDonald's Central America operator), and CARHCO (now Walmart Central America).

Sergio lives in Guatemala City with his wife, Paulina, and their four children.

sergio.paiz@grupopdc.com
www.grupopdc.com

www.ingramcontent.com/pod-product-compliance
Lightning Source LLC
LaVergne TN
LVHW022044200926
848481LV00003B/782